Cambridge Elements

Elements in Semantics
edited by
Jonathan Ginzburg
Université Paris-Cité
Daniel Lassiter
University of Edinburgh

TYPES AND THE STRUCTURE OF MEANING

Issues in Compositional and Lexical Semantics

Stergios Chatzikyriakidis
University of Crete

Robin Cooper
University of Gothenburg

Eleni Gregoromichelaki
University of Gothenburg

Peter R. Sutton
Potsdam University

Shaftesbury Road, Cambridge CB2 8EA, United Kingdom

One Liberty Plaza, 20th Floor, New York, NY 10006, USA

477 Williamstown Road, Port Melbourne, VIC 3207, Australia

314–321, 3rd Floor, Plot 3, Splendor Forum, Jasola District Centre,
New Delhi – 110025, India

103 Penang Road, #05–06/07, Visioncrest Commercial, Singapore 238467

Cambridge University Press is part of Cambridge University Press & Assessment,
a department of the University of Cambridge.

We share the University's mission to contribute to society through the pursuit of
education, learning and research at the highest international levels of excellence.

www.cambridge.org
Information on this title: www.cambridge.org/9781009619356

DOI: 10.1017/9781009285322

© Stergios Chatzikyriakidis, Robin Cooper, Eleni Gregoromichelaki
and Peter R. Sutton 2025

This publication is in copyright. Subject to statutory exception and to the provisions
of relevant collective licensing agreements, with the exception of the Creative Commons
version the link for which is provided below, no reproduction of any part may take place
without the written permission of Cambridge University Press & Assessment.

An online version of this work is published at doi.org/10.1017/9781009285322
under a Creative Commons Open Access license CC-BY-NC 4.0 which permits re-use,
distribution and reproduction in any medium for non-commercial purposes providing
appropriate credit to the original work is given and any changes made are indicated.
To view a copy of this license visit https://creativecommons.org/licenses/by-nc/4.0

When citing this work, please include a reference to the DOI 10.1017/9781009285322

First published 2025

A catalogue record for this publication is available from the British Library

ISBN 978-1-009-61935-6 Hardback
ISBN 978-1-009-28529-2 Paperback
ISSN 2754-0367 (online)
ISSN 2754-0359 (print)

Cambridge University Press & Assessment has no responsibility for the persistence
or accuracy of URLs for external or third-party internet websites referred to in this
publication and does not guarantee that any content on such websites is, or will
remain, accurate or appropriate.

For EU product safety concerns, contact us at Calle de José Abascal, 56, 1°, 28003
Madrid, Spain, or email eugpsr@cambridge.org.

Types and the Structure of Meaning

Issues in Compositional and Lexical Semantics

Elements in Semantics

DOI: 10.1017/9781009285322
First published online: May 2025

Stergios Chatzikyriakidis
University of Crete

Robin Cooper
University of Gothenburg

Eleni Gregoromichelaki
University of Gothenburg

Peter R. Sutton
Potsdam University

Author for correspondence: Stergios Chatzikyriakidis,
stergios.chatzikyriakidis@uoc.gr

Abstract: This Element addresses the role of structure in semantic analysis from the perspective of theories of meaning using rich theories of types. It also relates the theory of frames to these type theories as introducing, to some extent, similar structure into semantic analysis. The Element shows how a structured approach is necessary to appropriately analyze phenomena in areas as diverse as lexical semantics and the semantics of attitudinal constructions referring to psychological states. In particular, these are polysemy taken together with copredication, and attitudes such as belief and knowledge. The Element argues that the very same structure required to define a rich system of types enables us to adequately analyze both of these phenomena, thus revealing similarities in two otherwise apparently unrelated topics in semantics. It also argues that such theories facilitate a semantic theory oriented toward a psychological and contextually situated view of meaning. This title is also available as open access on Cambridge Core.

Keywords: structured semantic objects, type theory, frames, TTR, copredication, polysemy, propositional attitude constructions

© Stergios Chatzikyriakidis, Robin Cooper, Eleni Gregoromichelaki and Peter R. Sutton 2025

ISBNs: 9781009619356 (HB), 9781009285292 (PB), 9781009285322 (OC)
ISSNs: 2754-0367 (online), 2754-0359 (print)

Contents

1 The Nature of Structure in Semantics   1
2 Structure in the Attitudes   14
3 Structure in Polysemy and Copredication   27
4 Summary: Adding Structure to Semantics?   55

   References   59

1 The Nature of Structure in Semantics

In standard formal semantics deriving from the work of Montague (1974), comparatively little structure is used in the model theoretic domain. This is reflected in two ways:

- There are a small number of basic types.
- There is only one way of constructing new types: by forming the type of functions from the objects of one type to those of another type.

In Montague's formulation there are two basic types: e, for entities, and t, for truth-values (0 and 1). In addition to entities and truth-values, possible worlds and moments of time play a role as distinct kinds of objects in the type system. Otherwise, all the kinds of objects we need in order to do semantics are treated as some kind of function based on these basic elements. For example, one-place relations are functions from entities to truth-values (that is, the characteristic function of a set of entities); two-place relations are functions from entities to one-place relations; properties are functions from possible worlds and moments of time to one-place relations; and propositions are functions from possible worlds and moments of time to truth-values (that is, the characteristic function of a set of pairs each consisting of a possible world and a moment of time). This reductionist approach to the construction of semantic notions such as property and proposition is appealing for its economy and elegance. Nevertheless, there have been several proposals for adding other basic kinds of objects to Montague's ontology, such as stages, kinds, events and perspectives. For a recent discussion of issues in natural language ontology, see Liefke (2024).

The situation is very different in approaches based on what have been called *rich* theories of types deriving from the work of Martin-Löf (1984). Here, a richly structured semantic domain is introduced, reflected in the following ways:

- There is in principle no limit on the number of basic types that can be introduced.
- There is a large number of ways of constructing new types. Often the new types so constructed are themselves structured, in the sense that we can find and operate on the components that have been used to construct them.

The initial impression of such systems on a linguist trained in formal semantics can be one of overwhelming ontological promiscuity, a kind of richness that appears to make it difficult to construct the kind of restrictive linguistic theory that linguists are used to. Our aim in this Element is to explore this additional structure introduced by rich theories of types and suggest that it can provide advantages over the relatively unstructured approach we have inherited from Montague. Our strategy will be to look at two distinct areas which may at first appear to be unrelated:

- the semantics of attitude reports such as *Kim believes that Sam is in Japan*
- the treatment of polysemy in lexical semantics, for example *lunch* can mean either an event or the food which is eaten at a lunch event.

We will argue that the kind of structure provided by an approach based on a theory of types yields advantages in both of these cases. Our view is that the argument is made all the more powerful by the fact that the structure was not introduced to deal with either of these phenomena; rather, it was introduced as a way of treating the basic inferences with which type-theoretical approaches are concerned. Thus, the structure is an integral part of the logical approach which turns out to be applicable to widely different semantic phenomena. This suggests to us that this kind of approach is worthy of serious consideration as an alternative to the relatively unstructured approach to semantic domains which is taken in current mainstream formal semantics.

In the rest of this section we will first look at some different ways of introducing structure into semantics (Section 1.1). Then we look at type-theoretical approaches (Section 1.2). In Section 1.3 we introduce an approach to structure which has important correlations with certain kinds of type-theoretic approaches, namely frame theory and in Section 1.4 we make the relationship between frame theory and theories of types more explicit. Finally, in Section 1.5 we give an overview of the remaining sections in this Element.

1.1 Structure in Semantics

Since the beginning of formal semantics with Montague's seminal work in the early 1970s (Montague, 1974), various proposals have been presented for adding more structure to semantic analysis in order to achieve a better match with the psychologically motivated intuitions about meaning in language that speakers have and the practical ability that language users display when they deploy linguistic structures appropriately in meaning-involving situations ("sense-making", De Jaegher & Di Paolo, 2007). In general, there are two main strategies for adding structure. One is to take a proof-theoretic approach rather than a model-theoretic one. Here the aim is to relate natural language to a formal language and rigorously define inference in this language. Meaning is then seen as derived on the basis of judgements and inferential steps (actions, methods, programs) as defined in this language (see, e.g., Martin-Löf, 1982, 1996).

The characterisation of inference relies on the formal structure of the language and inference action rules and this means that meaning is defined in terms of this structure rather than structures occurring independently in a model-theoretic domain. This is the strategy pursued, for example, in the type-theoretic approach to natural language semantics as developed by Ranta (1994b).

On a model-theoretic approach there are two strategies for introducing structure, which can potentially be used together. One is to introduce an essential formal language which mediates between the natural language syntax and the model theory, that is, a formal language which is itself in need of model-theoretic interpretation. This is, for example, the strategy pursued in classical Discourse Representation Theory (DRT, Kamp & Reyle, 1993). We call this an *essential* formal language because it cannot be eliminated in the way that Montague's intensional logic (IL) can in Montague (1973), as discussed in the general framework set up in Montague (1970) (but cf. Muskens, 1996, where it is argued that DRT can be incorporated into Montague's general programme). This possibility of elimination was central to Montague's claim that natural language could be interpreted directly using the tools developed for model theories of formal logic (encapsulated in the slogan "English as a formal language" and illustrated in Montague, 1974). Part of the claim in the early work on DRT was that Montague's strategy did not extend to an account of discourse anaphora (but see Groenendijk & Stokhof, 1990, for an early suggestion for how discourse anaphora could be incoporated into a Montague-style approach).

The other way of introducing structure is to add structure to the semantic domain itself. One way to do this is to add more kinds of basic objects to the semantic domain (for example, Carlson's (1977) differentiation between kinds, individuals and stages among the entities in the semantic domain). Another way is to use objects in the semantic domain which are themselves structured, in the sense that they are made up of smaller elements, ideally, with significance attributed to the order or stages of their combination and defining relations or constraints between the different levels/stages of combination. For example, various proposals have been made for structured meanings, originally introduced by Lewis (1970), based on an idea by Carnap (1956), and developed by Cresswell (1985). Various other ideas for structured meanings or propositions have been introduced into the literature, starting perhaps with Russell's notion of a singular proposition in which worldly objects themselves ('things'), as well as 'concepts', are constituent parts (Russell, 1903; see also Soames, 1987).

These strategies for introducing structure are summarised in Figure 1. They are not mutually exclusive. For example, it would be possible to use several kinds of objects and structured objects in the semantic domain and to use both

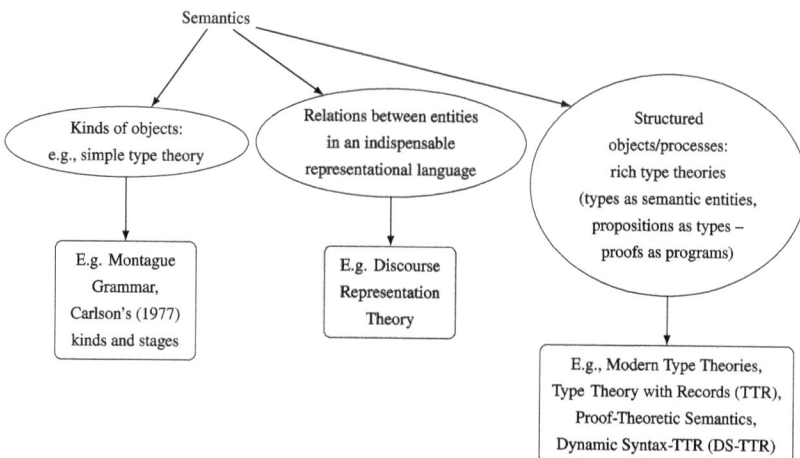

Figure 1 Strategies for introducing structure. Oval nodes represent theoretical commitments, and rectangular nodes are examples of theories with the theoretical commitments of their mothers.

an essential formal language and structure in the semantic domain (although a combination of these three is not attested to our knowledge, see Figure 1).

Also, when it comes to the aforementioned proof-theoretic–model-theoretic divide, there is no sharp distinction. Luo (2014) and Chatzikyriakidis and Luo (2020) argue that a Modern Type Theory (MTT) approach employs structure and is simultaneously proof theoretic and model theoretic with respect to natural language. On the other hand, we have purely model-theoretic semantics accounts in the tradition of Montague (1970, 1973) as well as purely Proof-Theoretic Semantics (PTS) accounts like Francez and Dyckhoff (2010) where natural language does not make contact with the world (see also Bekki, 2018). In MTT semantics (Chatzikyriakidis & Luo, 2020; Luo, 2011; Ranta, 1994a, 1994c), inference is defined through proof-theoretic rules and structures in the formal language of Constructive Type Theory, that is, without resorting to set theory. Thus, interpretation on a separate model structure is eliminated. But types and their inferential articulation captured through judgements (a form of formal epistemic action) play the role that set theoretic constructions play in Montague Semantics (e.g. the types of entities and situations). Approaches like Cooper (2023) also fall in between the purely model-theoretic and the purely proof-theoretic approaches. However, Cooper's theory is closer to purely model-theoretic accounts, as, even though some notions from proof-theory are maintained, these are defined in terms of operations on the structure of set-theoretic objects.

In this Element, we will focus on some current theories which do not use an intermediate essential formal language. This is either because the frameworks are proof-theoretic, with inference defined over the logical structure, and thus the logical representation is not seen as an intermediary to a model theory. Or an essential intermediary language is not needed because structured objects are directly defined within the semantic domain. We will present an account of this work and explain how it relates to the earlier work following the Montague tradition while at the same time offering us the possibility of a psychologically oriented but also situated theory of language use which could account for how linguistic meaning relates to our ability to perceive and interact with the world around us.

All the theories we discuss use structure directly in this way as part of their general strategy in the design of semantics rather than, say, just introducing structure for certain kinds of objects, for example centred propositions (Lewis, 1979, and much subsequent discussion). Proposals like Lewis' and structured meanings can be regarded as starting with analysis in terms of unstructured objects like possible worlds and then adding other objects to them (a centred possible world is, for example, a pair of a possible world and an individual) in order to introduce the structure required for the analysis.

We will look at type-theoretic approaches deriving from the work of Per Martin-Löf (1984; Nordström, Petersson & Smith, 1990) and the development of frame-based approaches to semantics deriving, on the one hand, from early linguistic work by Charles Fillmore (1976) and, on the other, from psychological work by Lawrence Barsalou (1992).

1.2 Type-Theoretical Approaches

The use of type theory for natural language semantics originated with Montague's use of Church's (1940) simple type theory. Simple type theory is essentially different from modern rich type theories in that it provides only basic types for individuals and truth values (or, in Church's original version, propositions) and functions based on these basic types. For example, if the basic types are e and t, then the type theory would include all the possible function types $(e \to e), (e \to t), (t \to e), (t \to t), (e \to (e \to t))$ and so on.[1] That is, for any two types T_1 and T_2, $(T_1 \to T_2)$ would also be included in the set of types. In Montague's type theory, additional basic types for time points and possible worlds were introduced into this regime. However, such simple type theories did not provide the rich assortment of types provided in modern type theories where intuitively a type can be any type of individual (such as *Dog*) or type of situation or event (such as *BoyHugsDog*, the type of event where a boy hugs

---

[1] Montague's (1973) original notation, which we will sometimes use, is $\langle e, e \rangle$, $\langle e, t \rangle$, $\langle t, e \rangle$, $\langle t, t \rangle$, $\langle e, \langle e, t \rangle \rangle$ etc.

a dog). Essential here has been the insight that the types can serve as propositions. Thus, *BoyHugsDog* can be considered true just in case there is an event of that type.

The first major application of Martin-Löf's modern type theory to the semantics of natural language[2] was Aarne Ranta's seminal book *Type-Theoretical Grammar* (Ranta, 1994b), and much of the subsequent work on type-theoretical approaches builds on or reacts to this work.

A few years after the publication of Ranta's book, Christian Retoré and colleagues began publishing on the use of linear logic for natural language syntax and in particular lexicalised grammars (Lecomte & Retoré, 1998, for example). This has led to several important works on the nature of the lexicon from a type-theoretic perspective, in particular dealing with aspects of Pustejovsky's Generative Lexicon (Asher & Pustejovsky, 2006; Bassac, Mery & Retoré, 2010; Retoré, 2014).

In the first decade of the twenty-first century, Luo began applying his type theory with *coercive subtyping* to the analysis of natural language semantics. This has led to a significant body of work on the type-theoretic approach to semantics, to a significant extent in collaboration with Chatzikyriakidis, culminating in their book Chatzikyriakidis and Luo (2020). Asher collaborated with Luo on the formalisation of coercions (in the sense of Pustejovsky) in Luo's type-theoretical framework (Asher & Luo, 2012), thus connecting back to some of the concerns of Retoré and colleagues, and Asher wrote a book (Asher, 2011) on coercions in lexical semantics, the nature of types, and category-theory connections.

Type Theory with Records (Cooper, 2023) is a theory of types inspired by Martin-Löf's type theory and subsequent work in the type theory community on record types. It differs from other approaches in that it is grounded in set theory and makes choices that are classical rather than intuitionistic. Part of the motivation for this is to connect it back to the classical model-theoretic approach in semantics, as found in Montague's semantics. The general TTR literature, however, takes a more explicitly cognitive approach than the Montague tradition, relating semantics to perception, action and affordances.

1.3 Frame-Theoretical Approaches

Fillmore (1976) introduces Frame Semantics in order to explicate the function of words as "tools" used by agents in a particular order and with particular goals. This he opposes to the aims of compositional semantics, which sees the

---

[2] Although Ranta (1988, 1991, 1994a, 1994c) and Sundholm (1986, 1989) represent significant earlier work.

structure of a sentence statically as a jigsaw of meaning pieces.[3] In an early attempt to blend the requirements of standard divisions of linguistic labour between semantics and pragmatics, Fillmore states that, in order to retrieve the meaning of an utterance, we have to understand the purposes of the agents who used the tools in this particular instance. Therefore, part of the motivation for Fillmore's Frame Semantics was to provide an account for how utterances are interpreted not only in terms of the information they directly encode but also as publicly available "categories of experience" (concepts, types in our construal) that are "underlain by a motivating situation" (Fillmore, 1976, p. 112) which grounds the knowledge required to be shared between situated agents in the presented categorisation of experience. As an example, Fillmore suggests that a common *commerce frame* can be activated in the mind of an addressee by the use of many expressions, including *buy*, *sell*, *pay*, *cost*, *spend* and *charge* (Fillmore, 1977, 1982). Suppose that this frame is activated in the mind of the addressee by the use of *bought* when someone utters *I bought an apple*. This not only fills in part of the commerce frame insofar as it conveys that the speaker purchased an apple at some past point but also activates a structure in which there is some seller, some place or point of sale, and some transaction of money and so on such that the activation of this frame may facilitate follow-up questions such as *From whom?*, *From where?* and *How much did it cost?*

In contrast to Fillmore's more communication-centred approach, Barsalou (1992) motivates frames cognitively, in part as an improvement upon the feature lists that were the common representational format of, for example, prototypes and exemplars. Frames, for Barsalou, are feature structures implemented as recursive attribute-value structures enriched with relations. Constraints between values and attributes can represent knowledge such as the correlation between an apple's skin colour and its level of sweetness.

Löbner (2014) and Petersen (2015) (among others) adopt Barsalou's conception of frames and propose that frames can be used as a common format for the representation of a large number of linguistic phenomena. For instance, rather than the flat prototype feature list for **apple** consisting of, for example, **red**, **sweet**, **round**, a frame for the prototype **apple** will consist of interconnected ATTRIBUTES (edges in a graph) and *values* (nodes), each of which is annotated with a **type**. For example in (1), **apple**, **skin**, **red** and **round** are types in a type hierarchy, where, for instance, **red** would be a subtype of **colour** and all types are subtypes of a general type τ. Attributes are then functions of type $\langle \tau, \tau \rangle$, where, say, SKIN applied to value v_1 of type **apple** returns value v_2 of type **skin**.

---

[3] Interestingly for our purposes, the notion of Fregean compositionality is also challenged by Constructive Type Theories in the Martin-Löf tradition (see, e.g., Martin-Löf, 1982, regarding lazy evaluation).

(1)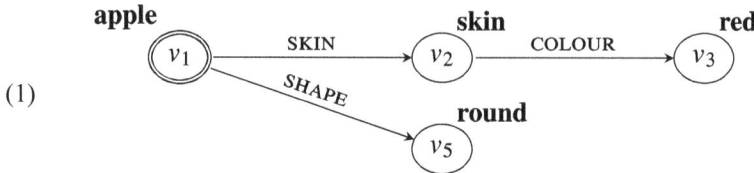

One feature of these frames (so-called Düsseldorf frames) that is not found in Barsalou's version is a *central node* that determines what that frame is a frame of (in extensional terms, its referent), for example indicated by the double ring around the **apple** node in (1). Notably, such frames stand for cognitive conceptual structure, decomposed with respect to lexical contents, that is, sublexical. They are argued to constitute mental representations rather than sociocultural public categories of experience and even assumed to be implemented by neuronal circuits (Petersen & Werning, 2007). In such frames, the main locus of structure is provided via graphs that can be presented as feature structures in recursive attribute-value matrix (AVM) notation. Frames as the semantic representations do not systematically add structure via directly enriching the type theory as, for example, MTT semantics and TTR. For this reason, they lack expressivity within the system to define logical operations like quantification as part of the semantic representation (see, e.g., Kallmeyer et al., 2015), while a separate syntactic formalism and linking mechanisms are needed to define the syntax–semantics interface.[4]

1.4 Type-Theoretic Characterisations of Frames

Although frames can be modelled as graph representations, they can also be modelled within a richer type theory, which has been pursued within TTR (Cooper, 2016, 2023). The relevant notions of TTR that are needed here are those of a *judgement* and a *record*. The typing judgement $a : T$ indicates (that an agent or a system performs the epistemic act of) classifying an object a as being of type T. For example, the concept of an apple can be captured by means of various judgements that attribute properties to an individual a during an observation of a situation s that provides the evidence or proof that a is an apple:[5]

---

[4] However, frame types as "first-class citizens" are introduced in Balogh and Osswald (2021). For a discussion of this see Gregoromichelaki et al., *Dialogical Interaction, Types, and the Structure of Meaning*, forthcoming, another volume in this series devoted primarily to type theoretical approaches to dialogue phenomena.

[5] Proofs can be taken to be implemented as programs in which case types correspond to packages of actions (*macros*) (as in, e.g., Gregoromichelaki et al., 2020).

(2) $a : Ind$
    $s : apple(a)$

Here, *Ind* is a basic type and apple(*a*) is a type constructed with the predicate 'apple'. These judgements concern a particular apple, *a*. In order to talk about a more general type of situation that contains *some* apple (that is, the type of all apple-containing situations), TTR uses *record types*. These are essentially pairings of *labels* and types. Each pairing of a label and a type is known as a *field* in the record type. In the record type in (3) the labels are 'x' and 'e'.

(3) $\begin{bmatrix} x & : & Ind \\ e & : & apple(x) \end{bmatrix}$

This record type can be instantiated by a *record*, intuitively modelling a situation in the world. The record has to contain fields with the same labels as those in the record type and objects in the fields which are of the types in the record type. Example (4) represents a record that is a witness for (3).

(4) $\begin{bmatrix} x & = & a \\ e & = & s \end{bmatrix}$
    where *a* is of type *Ind* and
    s is of type apple(*a*).

Note that the 'e'-field in (3) does not strictly contain a type. The 'x' in 'apple(x)' is not an individual but a label. This is a *dependent field* where the 'x' gets substituted for by whatever is in the 'x'-field in the record we are checking. Thus, in (4), *s* is checked for the type 'apple(*a*)' since *a* is the value in the 'x'-field in the record in (4).

An important aspect of record types is that a record may contain more fields than required by a type for which it is a witness. Consider, for example, the record in (5), which is like (4) except that it has an additional field labelled 'y' whose value, *b*, is of type *Ind*.

(5) $\begin{bmatrix} x & = & a \\ e & = & s \\ y & = & b \end{bmatrix}$

This is also of the type (3) since it meets the requirements on the 'x' and 'e'-fields. This means that record types introduce a notion of subtyping. In TTR *subsumption* is used for subtyping. This means that T_1 is a subtype of T_2 (written in TTR as $T_1 \sqsubseteq T_2$) just in case every witness for T_1 is also a witness for T_2.[6] Consider the type in (6) for which (5) would be a witness.

---

[6] Actually, the notion as defined in Cooper (2023) is stronger than this. It has to be necessarily (or provably) the case that if something is a witness for T_1 it is also a witness for T_2.

(6) $\begin{bmatrix} x & : & Ind \\ e & : & apple(x) \\ y & : & Ind \end{bmatrix}$

Any record of the type (6) will also be of the type (3). Thus, if we add an additional field to a record type, the new type will be a subtype of the original one. Furthermore, if we replace a type in a field in a record type with a subtype of that type, then the new record type will be a subtype of the original one. Finally, any type is a subtype of itself.

Records in TTR (used to model situations) are recursively defined sets of labelled values (*fields*, e.g. [$\ell = s$]) such that records can be the values of labels within a record, as in (7).

(7) $\begin{bmatrix} \ell_1 & = & [\ell_{1a}=e_1] \\ \ell_2 & = & e_2 \end{bmatrix}$

This means that, as in (8), record types are also recursively defined sets of labels and types (fields) with the additional advantage that these types may depend on values specified in the record.

(8) $\begin{bmatrix} \ell_1 & : & [\ell_{1a}:T_1] \\ \ell_2 & : & T_2 \end{bmatrix}$

We now model Düsseldorf frames by means of records and record types. This brings advantages from type theory to frame theory, for example that we can distinguish frames modelled as records, intuitively situations, from frame types (situation types) modelled as record types, a distinction that is less transparently indicated in Düsseldorf frame-theoretic approaches. Record types furthermore bring with them a notion of *subtyping*, commensurate with frame *subsumption* in Düsseldorf frame theory. This allows for initial underspecification and update of the types as perceived or expressed initially by an agent with subsequent refinement due to interaction with the sociomaterial environment. Additionally, TTR stays closer to the Montagovian semantic tradition insofar as formal composition is primarily driven by the tools of λ-calculus. For instance, the frame in (1) could be represented in TTR as in (9), a function from a record that witnesses an individual (of type *Ind*) to a more refined structured record type:

(9) $\lambda r: [x:Ind] . \begin{bmatrix} c_1 & : & apple(r.x) \\ c_2 & : & round(r.x) \\ y & : & Ind \\ c_3 & : & skin(r.x, y) \\ c_4 & : & red(y) \end{bmatrix}$

Record types in TTR can be considered as (structured) propositions following the propositions-as-types principle, discussed earlier. For instance, supplying the value *a* for the entity labelled x in the record in (9) would yield the proposition that *a* is a round apple with red skin (for more details about TTR, see Section 2). As such, TTR is a good instance of how frame-theoretic approaches and type-theoretic approaches are not mutually exclusive. Indeed, types that depend on values in records are a central part of the way that semantic composition is explained in TTR, although lexical decomposition has not been developed as far as in the Düsseldorf frames project (see, e.g., Osswald & Van Valin, 2014). This means that these two perspectives on semantics might benefit each other under a potential common approach.

Although Düsseldorf frame theory is psychologically oriented, based as it is on Barsalou's frame theory, frame semantics in the tradition of Fillmore, which has informed developments in TTR, also seeks to account for the cognitive and world-involving nature of language as used in context. We devote considerable attention to semantics, from a frame/type theoretic point of view, and cognition in Gregoromichelaki et al.[7]

1.5 The Structure of This Element

The rest of this Element is structured into two main sections, followed by a short summary section. The two main sections are centred on topics in semantics and pragmatics that we have chosen as a means of conveying what it is that the addition of structure contributes in terms of increased expressiveness, and, via this, providing analyses of phenomena that have proven highly challenging for less structured approaches.

In Section 2, we address a classic topic in propositional semantics, namely the relation between attributions of *propositional attitudes* via the relevant verbs and the propositions expressed by their complement clauses. For instance, we outline how structured semantics, both in terms of characterising belief contexts and in terms of taking types as intensional semantic entities, can be used to address the problems of possible world-based approaches: *logical omniscience* (we do not all believe every logical consequence of our beliefs), *hyper-intensionality* (not all logically equivalent propositions (e.g., tautologies, true mathematical propositions) intuitively have the same meaning) and *cross-modal anaphora* (the reference of anaphoric pronouns to non-existent entities across shared belief contexts).

---

[7] Forthcoming (see n. 4 for details).

In Section 3, we turn to *polysemy*, a topic in lexical semantics. We focus on some of the puzzles that arise for semantic theory from the fact that many expressions seem to have closely interrelated, albeit distinct, senses, that we can express more than one of these senses based on a single use of such expressions, and that the relations between these senses in terms of individuation can be highly constrained in quantificational contexts. For instance, in (10), intuitively, *carried back home* modifies physical books, and *read* applies to the informational contents of the books.

(10)   Alex carried back home and then read three books from the library.

Furthermore, (10) seems to require that there be three distinct physical books, each with distinct physical contents (it has been argued that the sentence would not be true if Alex brought home three copies of the same book), the *double-distinctness* reading (Gotham, 2017). Although such cases pose difficulties for semantic theories based upon the simply-typed λ-calculus, we show that a number of alternatives based upon a richer type theory can accommodate these data. Furthermore, we argue that double-distinctness readings require one to enrich the structure of the lexicon of, for example, common nouns such that they include individuation criteria (that can be modified in context), a finding that echoes similar conclusions drawn from work on the mass/count distinction.

Due to space limitations, we do not discuss a third topic which we originally had in mind for this Element, namely *dialogue*: a domain where both the analysis of the attitudes and the analysis of what is required for analysing enriched lexical meanings intersect. Instead, we discuss discuss dialogue in depth in another Element in this series (E. Gregoromichelaki, S. Chatzikyriakidis, R. Cooper and P. R. Sutton, Dialogical interaction, types, and the structure of meaning, Cambridge University Press, forthcoming). As a very brief overview, there we argue that in the domain of providing a plausible semantics for modelling language use in dialogue, arguably, we need an account of attitude ascription. Most frameworks assume that explaining both meaning and syntactic structure in conversation needs to make reference to structured objects that stand for the changing status of information in the cognitive states (beliefs or, more generally, *information states*) of the participants. Here the old distinctions between semantics and pragmatics break down as issues of underspecification and dynamic update are introduced in the heart of the semantic mechanisms that are needed to account for dialogue action interpretation and execution. In addition, the issue of polysemy and inferential derivation of the appropriate interpretation in context appears when we are confronted with making explicit the function of subsentential utterances ("fragments") in dialogue. For instance, the string *Lina* in *B*'s question is not intended to refer to a particular individual under the readings provided:

(11)   A: Did Lina leave?
        B: Lina?
        (i) Did you utter the word *Lina*?
        (ii) Who are you referring to with the name *Lina*?

The clarification question that *B* asks in (11) is underspecified with respect to, at least, the readings in (i) to (ii) and more (see, e.g., Ginzburg, 2012). The linguistic forms, contextual conditions and operations that give rise to such interpretations need to be defined over fine-grained structured semantic and syntactic objects and action sequences in order to resolve the interpretation of such fragments or elliptical structures (Ginzburg & Cooper, 2004). We review how the challenges of modelling such dialogue phenomena in their full but systematic complexity have motivated the addition of fine-grained structure to models of the context. Included are the interlocutors' belief states, their own and others' perspective on the common ground (belief attribution) and how these evolve under the structure imposed by the turn-taking system of conversation. Given that such modelling devices need to be fine-grained enough to include partial, dynamic and subpropositional syntactic and semantic constructs, modelling the grounding of conversational moves (i.e., negotiating and accepting/rejecting contributions to an exchange), including clarification requests like the ones in (11), requires irreducible levels of structure with means of keeping track and addressing heterogeneous information of various types.

     In such cases, the syntactic and the semantic articulations of utterances need to be developed hand-in-hand, which leads to the question whether evolving partially specified semantic objects need to be defined along with partially specified and evolving syntactic constructs. At this point, the issue of incremental structure building, long considered an external performance factor, seems to arise in a unified way for both syntax and semantic constraints and some of the frameworks we examine define them in parallel.

     In a more radical move, some work indicates that defining separate syntactic structure over strings of words is not only unmotivated and redundant but also contraindicated for the proper modelling of dialogue phenomena (e.g. Gregoromichelaki et al., 2011). Having unified semantics and pragmatics as manipulating a single vocabulary and integrated structures under type-theoretic assumptions, an attempt is being developed to subsume syntactic structuring to the functional requirements of conversation. This leads us to reconsider whether the distinction between form and meaning can be maintained if we take the view that structure in the world is picked up through language and conceptualisation, that conversational interaction organises structured language use and that, therefore, interaction shapes the constructs we need to analyse structure in natural languages and action coordination.

2 Structure in the Attitudes

In this section we will discuss some approaches to attitudes such as belief and knowledge which exploit structure relating to types and compare these with some other current theories of the attitudes which exploit structure either in the semantic models or in an intermediate or proof-theoretic representation. The word *attitude* is used in the literature to talk about attitudes that individuals may have to propositions. Thus, for example, the verb *believe* is traditionally construed as representing a relation between individuals and propositions as in (12) which expresses that Kim stands in the belief-relation to the proposition expressed by *Sam has gone to Japan*.

(12)   Kim believes that Sam has gone to Japan

Other examples of similar attitude verbs are *know*, *doubt* and *regret*. In this section, we will mainly concentrate on sentences reporting belief in line with much of the literature which sees belief as presenting basic problems of semantic analysis which are common to all the attitude verbs.

2.1 Belief States and Possible Worlds

The analyses of belief that have been presented can be divided according to two semantic design choices that can be made: (i) using *belief states*, that is, mental states corresponding to an individual having a certain belief and (ii) using *possible worlds*, the set of all logical possibilities for the way the world could be. Let us start with belief states.

The most common treatment of belief reports containing the verb *believe* in linguistic formal semantics does not make any explicit reference to a belief state. The belief relation between individuals and propositions is determined like any other relation in the model. That is, an n-place relation corresponds to a set of ordered n-tuples in the model and objects stand in the relation according to the model just in case they constitute an n-tuple in the relation. Thus, for the relation 'believe' this might be expressed as (13).

(13) $M \models \text{believe}(a, p)$ iff $\langle a_M, p_M \rangle \in \text{believe}_M$

This says that the model, M, makes 'believe(a,p)' true just in case the pair consisting of the individual that a represents in M and the proposition that p in M is a member of the set of ordered pairs represented in the model by 'believe'. The analysis of belief reports given by Montague (1973) is of this kind. For Montague, propositions were modelled as sets of possible worlds.[8] In contrast to this, Hintikka (1962) presents an analysis in which the belief state of the believer *is* represented. For Hintikka, any agent, a, is associated with a set of belief-worlds. This is the set of possible worlds in which the propositions that a believes are true. The basic truth condition for a belief-sentence on this approach is expressed informally in (14).

(14) a believes p iff p is true in all of a's belief worlds

We see from this that there are two potential roles for possible worlds in the analysis of belief. One is in the modelling of propositions as sets of possible worlds and the other is in the modelling of belief states as sets of possible worlds. In what follows we will look at some analyses of belief where the choice is made not to use possible worlds in either of these ways, thus resolving the second design choice mentioned earlier in a different way. The motivation for avoiding possible worlds is given by a number of problems that have been pointed out in the philosophical and linguistic literatures. A recent summary with references is given, for example, by Cooper (2023, ch. 6). The problems concern possible worlds considered as total universes, that is, ways in which the whole universe could be which would determine truth or falsity for any proposition we might consider.[9] The problems are of two kinds: those which concern the nature of possible worlds themselves and those which concern the proposal to model propositions as sets of possible worlds. The first kind of problem involves how to individuate and count possible worlds if, as is normally assumed, space and time are based on the real numbers. For any world in which a given object is at a given location in space and time, there is another world in which that object is at another location. This means that there are at least as many possible worlds as there are real numbers. Intuitively, we should be able to distinguish two possible worlds by finding a proposition that is true in one of them but not in the other. But we have no reliable way of distinguishing between two possible worlds, since we cannot enumerate all the propositions that could be used to distinguish them. This problem is compounded if our

---

[8] Actually, sets of pairs of possible worlds and moments of time, but we will ignore this complication here.
[9] The term "possible world" is also often used (for example in probability theory) to refer to a way part of the universe could be, that is, they would only determine truth or falsity for a proper subset of the set of all propositions we might consider.

theory of propositions involves modelling them as sets of possible worlds. We cannot simultaneously model propositions as sets of possible worlds in which they are true and possible worlds as sets of propositions which are true in them. Furthermore, modelling propositions as sets of possible worlds does not seem to distinguish all the propositions we need. Consider the sentences in (15).

(15)   a.   The glass was half full
        b.   The glass was half empty

These must be true in exactly the same possible worlds and yet they do not seem to represent the same proposition. For example, we can be glad about (15a) and not glad about (15b).

In summary, the problems with possible worlds seem to be that there are too many of them for reasoning about them to be tractable and that, nevertheless, the power set of possible worlds fails to provide enough propositions to make intuitive distinctions between propositions. Possible worlds thus fail to provide a straightforward account of propositions.

2.2 Rich Types, Contexts and Belief States

Ranta (1994b) presents the classic treatment of belief in the type-theoretical approach. It does not use possible worlds and it exploits the notion of *context* in type theory to model belief states. Thus, while, like Hintikka, it gives an explicit account of mental states, it does not use possible worlds to do this. A context in the Martin-Löf type theory that Ranta is using is a sequence of hypotheses of the form (16) (Ranta, 1994b, p. 89).

(16) $x_1 : T_1, x_2 : T_2(x_1), \ldots, x_n : T_n(x_1, \ldots, x_{n-1})$

Here, $x_1, \ldots, x_n$ are variables and $T_i(x_j, \ldots, x_k)$ represents that the type T_i possibly depends on the values of the variables $x_j, \ldots, x_k$. It is usual to use the variables Γ and Δ for such contexts. The notion of context, here, is based on the use of assumptions in proof theory. In (17) we give a simplified version of an example that Ranta gives on p. 90.

(17) $$\frac{T : \textit{Type} \quad (x : T) \quad P(x) : \textit{Type}}{(\Sigma x : T)P(x) : \textit{Type}}$$

Here, the first premise says that T is a type (it is of the type *Type*). As an example, T might be the type *Boy*, the type of boys. The second premise is that, given a context where $x : T$, we can conclude that $P(x) : \textit{Type}$, that is, $P(x)$ is a type. As an example, P might be *Run*, which could be construed as a function which for any boy, x, will return a type, $Run(x)$, which could be thought of as the type of situations in which x runs (cf. the discussion of TTR earlier in Section 1.4). The second premise is then a conditional premise which could be paraphrased as "for any x, if $x : T$, then $P(x) : Type$". The conclusion in (17) tells us of a new type that can be constructed given that the premises hold. This example involves a Σ-type which, following our exemplification of T and P, would be $(\Sigma x : Boy)Run(x)$, which could be thought of intuitively as the type of situations in which some boy runs. Note that (17) does not tell us that there is a boy that runs; rather, it tells us of the existence of the Σ-type. Its import as a type corresponding to existential quantification would be given by other inference rules in the system. Note that the types we are discussing here can be naturally construed as propositions as mentioned in Section 1.2. Supposing that $j : Boy$, then the type $Run(j)$ can do double duty as the proposition that j runs. It is true just in case there is a situation of the type $Run(j)$.

It is important that such hypotheses or assumptions as $x : T$ have variables since the premise is meant to hold for anything which could be assigned to x. Contexts in type theory can be used to express that propositions are true in a given context. Ranta's illustration is (18), which he glosses as "$T(x_1,\ldots,x_n)$ is true in the context Γ".

(18) $T(x_1,\ldots,x_n)$ true (Γ)

An alternative way of writing (18) is (19) (see, e.g, Chatzikyriakidis & Luo, 2020).

(19) $\Gamma \vdash T(x_1,\ldots,x_n)$ true

Ranta's insight is that contexts of this form can be used to model the hypotheses, or beliefs, that an agent has or is currently focussing on. Thus, the beliefs of a particular agent, A, can be represented as in (20).

(20) $\Gamma_A = x_1 : T_1,\ldots,x_n : T_n(x_1,\ldots,x_{n-1})$

The basic intuition is that a judgement that A believes a judgement J corresponds to the hypothetical judgement $\Gamma_A \vdash J$. Suppose that Γ_A is of the form (21).

(21) $\Gamma_A = \ldots,x_i : Boy, x_j : Run(x_i),\ldots$

It would follow from any instantiation of Γ_A that the type $(\Sigma x : Boy)Run(x)$ is true, that is, that there is some situation of the type. It would be the situation corresponding to the variable x_j in the context. Thus, (22) holds.

(22) $\Gamma_A \vdash (\Sigma x : Boy)Run(x)$

That is, (22) fulfils the condition for A believing that some boy runs.

2.3 Addressing the Logical Omniscience Problem

2.3.1 Actual Belief States as Contexts

One immediate consequence of thinking of beliefs as having the structure of contexts in this way is that we have two notions of belief, which Ranta calls *actual belief* and *potential belief* (Ranta, 1994b, p. 154, building on a distinction made on p. 91). The actual beliefs of A are those judgements which actually occur in A's belief context, Γ_A, that is, one of the judgements $x_1 : T_1$ or $x_i : T_i(x_1, \ldots, x_{i-1})$. Potential beliefs are those judgements which follow from Γ_A using the rules of type theory. Thus, given our earlier example, $(\Sigma x : Boy)Run(x)$ would be a potential belief, unless this type were associated with a variable somewhere else in Γ_A. There could be an alternative, as in (23).

(23) $\Gamma_A = \ldots, x_i : (\Sigma x : Boy)Run(x), \ldots$

In this case the belief would be actual. One could imagine using Ranta's distinction to analyse a phenomenon often considered to be pragmatic, namely, the difference between specific and non-specific indefinites. *Specific indefinites* are those where the believer has a particular variable associated with the type corresponding to the common noun, as in (21). *Non-specific indefinites* are cases like (23) where the believer only has the quantificational Σ-type associated with a variable. Such a distinction does not correspond to a difference in the world as such; rather, it corresponds to a difference in the structure of the agent's belief context. This kind of distinction seems hard to model in terms of the standard view of possible worlds, whether they are used to model propositions or belief states.

By concentrating on actual beliefs in our analysis of belief reports, we can avoid the problem of *logical omniscience*, which causes difficulties for the epistemic logic approach to belief as presented by Hintikka (1962), as discussed earlier. A consequence of saying that an agent believes all and only those propositions which are true in all of the agent's belief worlds is that agents automatically believe all the logical consequences of their beliefs. If a proposition is true in a possible world then all of its logical consequences will also be true in that possible world. This is because we are considering those worlds which are logically possible and we would not want to say that a world in which some logical consequence does not hold is logically possible. The problem, of course, is that human agents do not believe all the logical consequences of their beliefs. It is thus an advantage of Ranta's proposal that there is a way of avoiding this problem.

However, as Chatzikyriakidis and Luo (2020) correctly point out, Ranta's actual characterisation of the belief operator requires that A believes T just in case $\Gamma_A \vdash T$ *true*, that is, just in case *T follows* from *A*'s belief context, which means that it includes both actual and potential beliefs in Ranta's terms. Chatzikyriakidis and Luo (2020, ss. 4.5.3–4.5.4) introduce predicates which correspond to, in Ranta's terms, accessing the actual judgements in the context since they are predicates which hold of all and only the elements of the context but not in general of anything following from the context.

In these treatments, the introduction of structured contexts is being used to avoid the problem of logical omniscience which was introduced by Hintikka's analysis of belief in terms of sets of unstructured possible worlds considered as atoms. It is interesting to note that a treatment of belief such as that of Montague (1973) partially avoids logical omniscience by analysing belief not in terms of Hintikka's belief worlds but rather in terms of propositions, construed as sets of possible worlds.[10] Thus, if we were to represent the set of beliefs of an agent corresponding to a type-theoretical context (something which, of course, Montague does not do), it would be a set of *sets* of possible worlds, where each of the possible worlds is an unstructured atom. According to this view, a proposition q follows from a proposition p just in case every world in which p is true is one in which q is true, that is, modelling propositions as sets of possible worlds, as: $p \subseteq q$. If we treat belief, as Montague does, in terms of a relation between an agent, A, and a proposition, p, it does *not* follow that if A stands in the belief-relation to p, then A will stand in the belief-relation to any superset of p. This, however, is only a partial solution to the logical omniscience problem. The other part of the problem involves logically equivalent propositions which become identical because they are modelled as the same set of possible worlds. This is a problem which has been much discussed in the literature, recently, among others, by Chatzikyriakidis and Luo (2020) and Cooper (2023, ch. 6). It means that if you believe one true mathematical proposition (true in all possible worlds), such as *the sum of two with itself is four*, then you believe all true mathematical propositions (including, for example, Fermat's last theorem, proved relatively recently). As Cooper points out, it also means that if it was illegal that Kim sold the house to Sam then it was also illegal that Sam bought the house from Kim, assuming that we treat *illegal* as a predicate of propositions. Yet, there is a clear intuition that the selling could be illegal while the buying was legal. One might try to argue against this by saying that *illegal* is not really a predicate of the proposition that Kim sold the house to Sam or the proposition that Sam bought the house from Kim, for example, by saying that what is illegal is having the property of selling the house as opposed to having the property of buying the house. While it seems to be reasonable to

---

[10] Technically, sets of world-time pairs, as mentioned earlier.

say that illegal is related to properties in this way, we are still left with the puzzle of examples which seem to show that it can be a predicate of propositions as well as shown by a compositional treatment of examples like those in (24).

(24)   a.   It was illegal that Kim sold the house to Sam
        b.   Kim sold the house to Sam. That was illegal
        c.   That Kim sold the house to Sam was judged to be illegal

In (25) are some examples similar to (24a) which are not constructed.

(25)   a.   It feels illegal that pancake day isn't in February this year (https://twitter.com/aldiuk/status/1496062240990146560, retrieved 29/1, 2022)
        b.   On 2 March 2017, the Federal Administrative Court ruled that, in extreme circumstances, it was illegal that an agency denied access to life-ending substances. (https://en.wikipedia.org/wiki/Legality_of_euthanasia, retrieved 29/1, 2022)

Another strategy for approaching this problem (one taken by Parsons, 1990) is to say that buying and selling events are distinct events which always co-occur. A frame-based representation of this is to assume that *buy* and *sell* are subsumed under a shared commerce frame that is triggered by different verbs, for example, where *buy* and *sell* may be represented by the same frame that differs only with respect to the central node (on the assumption that buying and selling eventualities are non-identical by virtue of having discrete values for their thematic roles). For instance, a possible (partial) representation of the commerce frame is given in (26). We suppress values and leave the central node unspecified:

(26)

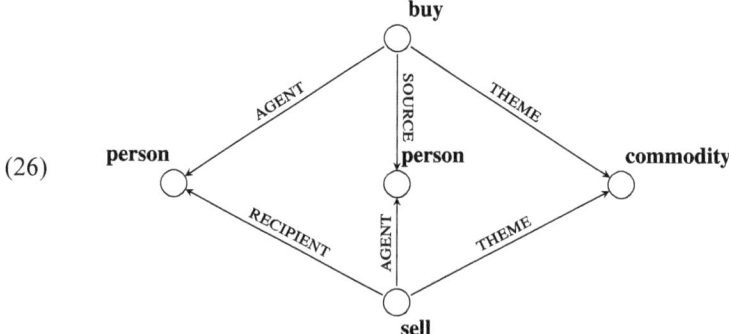

Parsons' main argument (p. 84) is based on the adverbials in the sentences in (27).

(27) a. Kim bought a tricycle from Sheehan with his MasterCard
      b. Sheehan sold a tricycle to Kim with his MasterCard

This argument that there are two events relies on a neo-Davidsonian approach to the modifier *with his MasterCard*. Thus, the neo-Davidsonian account involves analysing (27a) in terms of there being a buying event which occurred with Kim's MasterCard. From this it does not follow that there is a selling event with Kim's MasterCard. Therefore the buying event and the selling event must be distinct. This has to do with the neo-Davidsonian claim that all adverbial modifiers are predicates of events rather than modifiers of properties represented by verb phrases like *bought a tricycle from Sheehan*.[11] If you have a type system which allows higher types and also allows events to be of more than one type, then it is straightforward to treat the adverbial as a predicate modifier and claim that selling events are also buying events. Thus, this kind of problem can be solved in a type system which allows equivalent types which are not identical (i.e., types are *intensional*). In such a system (28a) does *not* imply (28b).

(28) a. for any a, $a : T_1$ iff $a : T_2$
      b. $T_1 = T_2$

In this way, a type system can add more structure to a semantic universe than would be possible in one based on sets of possible worlds, and the structure it adds has different consequences than the kind of structure added by introducing a neo-Davidsonian event semantics.

Ranta's approach, however, needs something more than we have mentioned so far if we are to model *de re* beliefs, that is, beliefs which the agent has about a particular object (cf. also the notion of Russellian singular propositions mentioned in Section 1). Since the notion of context is inspired by the notion of hypothesis as used in proof theory, exemplified in (17), the judgements in the context contain variables. Thus, (29a) expresses that A has a belief that there is a woman, whereas in order to represent that A has a belief that concerns a specific individual, Kim, say, represented by the constant k, we need instead a judgement of the form used in (29b).

(29) a. $\Gamma_A = \ldots, x_i : Woman, \ldots$
      b. $\Gamma_A = \ldots, x_i = k : Woman, \ldots$

Ranta (1994b, p. 152) calls the judgement in (29b) an anchoring of the belief that there is a woman. Chatzikyriakidis and Luo (2015b) discuss

---

[11] Davidson (1969/1980) himself defended a coarse-grained view of event identity, so would not necessarily accept the neo-Davidsonian conclusions about buying and selling (see, e.g., s. 8.3 in Parsons, 1990 for discussion).

examples such as (29b) as related to *manifest entries* in *signatures*, where they take the notion of signature from the Edinburgh Logical Framework (Harper, Honsell & Plotkin, 1993). Such manifest entries characterise the types of constants as opposed to variables. For a detailed discussion of signatures and contexts from a linguistic perspective, see Chatzikyriakidis and Luo (2020).

2.3.2 A Type-Theoretical Frame-Based Approach

Cooper (2023, ch. 6) presents a theory of attitudes which can be seen as a development from Ranta's proposal. Cooper's approach does not use type-theoretic contexts or signatures as such but rather records and record types. The correspondence between contexts of the kind Ranta discusses and record types is easy to see. For example, a context of the form (30a) corresponds to a record type of the form (30b).

(30)   a. $x_1 : T_1, \ldots, x_n : T_n(x_1, \ldots, x_{n-1})$

b. $$\begin{bmatrix} \ell_1 & : & T_1 \\ & \vdots & \\ \ell_n & : & T_n(\ell_1, \ldots, \ell_{n-1}) \end{bmatrix}$$

As briefly mentioned earlier in Section 1.4, a record type in TTR is a set of ordered pairs (called *fields*) consisting of a label and a type (which may itself be a record type).[12] The witnesses of record types are records which are similarly ordered pairs of labels and witnesses for the correspondingly labelled types in the record type. A record that witnesses a record type may in addition have fields with labels not occurring in the record type. A record which is a witness for a type like (30b) could be regarded as an anchoring for Ranta's context. Note that the *labels*, ℓ_i, in the record type are playing a similar role to the *variables*, x_i, in that context. In Cooper's terminology, a record type of the form (30b) would be regarded as a *context type* and the witness would be a *context* of that type. If we want a type to correspond to manifest entries in a context or signature as illustrated in (29b), we can use manifest fields in record types. A manifest field $\begin{bmatrix} \ell=a:T \end{bmatrix}$ requires that any witness for the record type have a in its field labelled by ℓ and that $a : T$. The use of manifest fields is illustrated in (31).

(31) $$\begin{bmatrix} \vdots \\ \ell_i=k & : & Woman \\ \vdots \end{bmatrix}$$

This allows us to represent a context type which is partially anchored.

---

[12] This is a simplified account for expository purposes. For a detailed account, see Cooper (2023).

Recasting Ranta's idea that contexts are used to represent an agent's beliefs in Cooper's terms means that now the beliefs are modelled as record types (used to model what Cooper would call a context type). This move gives us a direct characterisation of when a belief is true. It is true just in case the type which models it is true, that is, has a witness. Also, if we follow the "propositions as types" dictum, then we have a direct structured representation of the propositions that the agent believes. In the TTR treatment proposed by Cooper, an agent, A, whose beliefs are the type Bel_A, believes a type (proposition), T, just in case there is a relabelling of T, T_η, such that Bel_A is a subtype of T_η. On this approach, the labels used in T are not relevant to determining belief, although the labels are important in analysing anaphora. For example, suppose that Kim believes that some woman is a conductor. Kim's beliefs might be represented as a record type of the form (32) (see Cooper, 2023, for discussion of this kind of representation).

(32) $$\begin{bmatrix} \vdots \\ id_i : \begin{bmatrix} x : Ind \\ e : woman(x) \end{bmatrix} \\ id_j : \begin{bmatrix} e : conductor(\Uparrow id_i.x) \end{bmatrix} \\ \vdots \end{bmatrix}$$

(The $\Uparrow$ is a convenient notation which indicates that the path '$id_i.x$' is to be found in the next level up in the record type.)

Now suppose that an utterance of *Kim believes that some woman is a conductor* is assigned the content (33).

(33) $$\begin{bmatrix} e : believe(kim, \begin{bmatrix} x : Ind \\ c : woman(x) \\ e : conductor(x) \end{bmatrix}) \end{bmatrix}$$

According to the analysis given in Cooper (2023), (33) will be "true" (that is, there will be a record of this type) just in case there is a way of relabelling (34) so that (32) is a subtype of the relabelling.

(34) $$\begin{bmatrix} x : Ind \\ c : woman(x) \\ e : conductor(x) \end{bmatrix}$$

The relevant relabelling is represented by (35a) and the result of this relabelling is given in (35b), which is a supertype of (32).

(35) a. $x \rightsquigarrow id_i.x$
$c \rightsquigarrow id_i.e$
$e \rightsquigarrow id_j.e$

b. $\begin{bmatrix} id_i & : & \begin{bmatrix} x & : & Ind \\ e & : & woman(x) \end{bmatrix} \\ id_j & : & \begin{bmatrix} e & : & conductor(\Uparrow id_i.x) \end{bmatrix} \end{bmatrix}$

Cooper (2023) gives a detailed discussion of the relabelling mechanism which we will not repeat here. It should be clear from what we have said, though, that whatever labelling we had started with in (34), we would have been able to find a relabelling similar to (35a) that would justify the report on Kim's belief. Thus, the actual labelling of the belief corresponding to the complement of the sentence is not relevant to determining the truth of the utterance.

While the exact labelling used is not important for determining the truth of belief reports in this way, the labels, or variables in a context, are important for establishing anaphoric relations by using pronouns to reference the labels or variables. Ranta (1994b) gives an analysis of the intentional identity cases introduced by Geach (1967). These are cases where there appears to be anaphoric relatedness across the belief states of different agents without a requirement that there actually exist the kind of individual that the agents believe in. Geach's example is *Hob thinks a witch has blighted Bob's mare, and Nob wonders whether she (the same witch) killed Cob's sow*. The essential intuition behind Ranta's analysis is that there is a belief context which Hob and Nob share, namely one which requires there to be a witch. By having Hob's and Nob's belief contexts overlap with respect to the witch, we can indicate that they have different beliefs about the "same" witch, that is, indexed by the same variable in their respective belief contexts. Note that this alignment of their mental states does not in any way require that there be such a witch in the world. Geach's sentence is consistent with there being no such thing as a witch.

Cooper (2023) uses alignment of labelling in record types to similar effect and introduces a notion of point of view on another agent's belief state. This involves aligning record types in terms of their labels but introducing different facts in the point of view. An example he discusses is where two agents can have different names for the same (possibly non-existent) individual and being able to report a belief about the individual using names from either point of view. Thus, a Roman may report that Alexander, a Greek, believes that Zeus is chief of the gods or that he believes that Jupiter is chief of the gods, using the name in the Roman point of view, even though Alexander himself would not use this name. The identity of Zeus and Jupiter does not require that there exists a god with these names, just that there are appropriately aligned belief states.

Modelling belief states as types in this way provides solutions to a number of puzzles involving reference such as Frege's morning star/evening star, Kripke's Paderewski and Pierre and Geach's Hob/Nob. See Cooper (2023) for discussion.

There are two aspects of structure which are important for the kind of analysis that models belief states as types or contexts in the sense of Ranta. Firstly, we need to have a theory which includes a notion of mental state against which belief reports can be matched. Secondly, these mental states must have enough structure to make it possible to align them in an appropriate way. This is provided in the examples we have discussed by the variables in context or the labels in record types. It seems that without this kind of structure, cases of intentional identity are mysterious, as Geach originally pointed out.

2.3.3 Comparison with Other Approaches

These analyses coming from type theory are closely related to proposals that have been made in the framework of DRT. These include Kamp (1990), Kamp, van Genabith and Reyle (2011), Maier (2017) and Pross (2014) and more recently in what has come to be known as MSDRT (Mental State Discourse Representation Structure) as set out, for example, by Kamp (2022). This approach is similar to the type theory approach in exactly the required aspects of structure that we have pointed to. Mental states are modelled in the theory as discourse representation structures which contain the required indexing of structure using discourse referents. Mental states can be aligned by aligning discourse referents. It differs from what we have discussed here in that it has a commitment to a structured discourse representation structure (DRS) language rather than a structured semantic domain (see Figure 1) as such and it lacks the general inferential power normally invested in type-theoretical approaches, such as sub-typing.

One aspect of using the structure provided by theories of types for the analysis of attitude reports is that it does not involve any additional structure beyond that introduced in the types for the analysis of propositions and inference independently of the attitude reports and other intensional constructions. There are many proposals in the literature which introduce structure in addition to the basic notion of proposition in order to be able to deal with intensionality. Such proposals can either involve changing the notion of proposition or interpreting attitude reports in terms of unstructured propositions and some other element which provides more structure, such as a guise or a mode of presentation (see Kratzer, 2022, for a discussion and defence of this alternative). Important among these is the tradition of *structured meanings* in formal semantics beginning with Lewis (1970) based on the notion of *intensional isomorphism* introduced by Carnap (1956) and developed by Cresswell (1985). The idea here is that in addition to propositions as sets of possible worlds, we also keep a record of the interpretation of the syntactic constituents of the interpreted expression which are used to define the proposition. The same proposition can be constructed in different ways, which gives us a finer grain than the proposition on its own, and we can think of propositional attitudes as relations between individuals and pairings of propositions and structures essentially similar to the syntactic structure except with interpretations associated with their nodes rather than expressions of the language. One challenge for this kind of approach is that you do not get structure associated with synonymous lexical items. Thus, for example, the nouns *groundhog* and *woodchuck* are synonymous and yet people who do not know this can believe something about a groundhog without believing the same thing about a woodchuck. Another challenge is that there may be different constructions for which we would want to say not only that they are logically equivalent but that it is difficult to imagine somebody believing one but not the other. For example, any speaker of English who believes that Sam gave the book to Kim would be expected to believe that Sam gave Kim the book. Thus, structure of this kind does not immediately get us the kind of differentiation of propositions which would cover all we need for propositional attitudes.

2.4 Summary

In this section we have discussed approaches to the attitudes exploiting the kind of structure found in type theory. Ranta's approach uses contexts from type theory to represent belief states and defines what it means for an agent to have a belief in terms of what follows from the belief state, or, in the case of what Ranta calls actual beliefs, what items are contained in the belief context. This kind of structural approach enables us to deal with problems of hyperintensionality and intentional identity. Cooper's analysis can be seen as developing from Ranta's, though using record types in place of contexts. Since record types can also serve as propositions (following the propositions as types view), we get an immediate characterisation of what it means for a belief to be true. By the use of relabelling of record types, we see that the precise labels chosen for a record type are irrelevant for the belief attribution although they are relevant when it comes to determining anaphoric relations, in particular cases of intentional identity and other referential puzzles.

3 Structure in Polysemy and Copredication

As outlined in Section 1, on a Fillmorean conception of a frame, the same frame may underpin the way we understand multiple related expressions. For example, one frame could characterise a situation which would count from one perspective as a selling event and from another perspective as a buying event. (See the discussion of the commerce frame and event individuation in Section 2.3.) A natural extension of this idea is to apply it to at least some cases of *polysemy*, that is, to a certain kind of ambiguity in which a single lexical item can be used to express closely interrelated senses (we give a more detailed characterisation of polysemy in Section 3.1.1). For instance, *lunch* is standardly taken to be a polysemous expression. It can be used to talk about a lunch-eating event, but also the food that is eaten:

(36)   a.   Lunch was delicious.   [Description of food]
         b.   Lunch starts at noon.   [Description of an event]

We could therefore have a Fillmorean frame with participants for, say, an animate individual (the lunch eater) and some food, where under one conception the agent's interaction with the food is foregrounded (the eating) and in another the food itself is more prominent. Via introducing this frame, the meaning of *lunch* could be seen as facilitating either, or possibly also both, of these perspectives. As we shall show, compelling arguments have been made to suggest that a semantics based upon a system of simple types is insufficient to accommodate such data. Type-theoretical and frame-based approaches, in contrast, arguably have resources to accommodate the polysemy data via the modelling of different perspectives on the denotation of a polysemous expression, a topic we will explore in this section.

In Section 3.1, we lay out what we assume to be the characteristics of polysemy and we discuss a particular feature afforded by polysemous expressions, namely, *copredication*, in which a single use of a polysemous expression may license uses of multiple predicates, each of which targets a different sense of that expression. In Sections 3.2 and 3.3 we review some of the reactions in the semantics literature to two puzzles relating to polysemy. We argue that the first puzzle provides a strong basis for adopting a type system that is richer than that of the simply-typed λ-calculus, at least with respect to requiring more than just a functional type constructor. The second puzzle, which is based upon the interaction between polysemous expressions with quantifiers (including adjectival quantifiers such as numerals), we argue, provides a reason for enriching one's lexical semantic representations, minimally, to include individuation information as well as information about what the expression denotes. As we

3.1 Introducing Polysemy and Copredication
3.1.1 Polysemy versus Lexical Ambiguity and Coercion

In this section, in order to better clarify what is meant by *polysemy*, we briefly consider two other related phenomena: lexical ambiguity and coercion. In very broad terms, lexical ambiguity occurs when a single form has two, possibly unrelated, meanings,[13] while coercion (also known as *selectional polysemy*, Pustejovsky 2008) relates to when an expression can be used to express some sense, but only in the context of some other expression being used to modify it with incompatible sectional restrictions. Finally, the focus of this chapter, *polysemy* (also known as *complementary polysemy*, Pustejovsky, 1995; Weinreich, 1964 and *inherent polysemy*, Pustejovsky 2008) is roughly when a single form is associated with two closely related senses.

Polysemy, lexical ambiguity and the variety of readings one can get from an expression as a result of *coercion* are phenomena that are closely related and can be hard to separate insofar as, between the clear cases, there are more borderline instances of these categories. We start by comparing lexical ambiguity and polysemy. One example of a lexically ambiguous expression in English is *party*. It can be used to refer to a celebration, a political faction or a group (especially one that travels together).

(37)   a.   The party last night was wild.
         b.   The party elected yet another new leader.
         c.   The party set off at dawn.

In contrast, *statement* is a polysemous expression in English. It can be used to refer to an event (that of someone making a statement), to a physical object (a written or recorded artefact) and to information (the contents of the stating event or the written or recorded artefact).

(38)   a.   Alex's statement lasted half an hour.
         b.   Alex's statement is in the filing cabinet.
         c.   Alex's statement was not entirely true.

Insofar as both lexical ambiguity and polysemy involve expressions with multiple senses, the phenomena are related to one another. However, there is also

---

[13] As noted by Pustejovsky (1995), lexical ambiguity has also been described by Weinreich (1964) as *contrastive polysemy*.

a sense in which the phenomena are distinct. For instance, the senses of *party* seem to be only loosely related (all involve some plurality of people, but the people are not the referents of all senses of *party*). The senses for *statement*, in contrast, are more tightly related. Given the inherent vagueness in how closely senses are related to one another, we doubt that any categorical distinction can be made between lexical ambiguity and polysemy; however, at least for clear cases, there are distinctions that can be made. For instance, if an ambiguous expression has multiple senses in one language, these senses are not usually attested as being lexicalised by the same expression crosslinguistically.[14] For example, the three senses expressed by *party* in English are expressed by distinct expressions in German, namely, *Feier* ('party viz. celebration'), *Partei* ('political party') and *Reisegruppe* ('travel group'), respectively. In contrast, the senses of a polysemous expression in one language are more likely to be reflected by a single expression in another language.[15] This is what we find for *statement* in English (38) and *Stellungnahme* in German (39), in which the evidence for the different senses of *statement* and *Stellungnahme* is provided by modifiers. For instance, *lasted half an hour* in (38a) suggests the event-denoting sense of *statement*, *is in the filing cabinet* in (38b) the physical object sense and *is true* in (38c) the informational content sense. Similar considerations apply to *hat eine halbe Stunde gedauert*, *ist in dem Umschlag* and *ist sachlich* for *Stellungnahme* in (39).

(39) Die Stellungnahme hat eine halbe Stunde gedauert / ist in dem
      the statement   has a half hour   lasted   / is in the
      Umschlag / ist sachlich.
      envelope / is factual
      'The statement lasted half an hour/is in the envelope/is factual'

Having compared polysemy with lexical ambiguity, we now turn to a comparison between polysemy and another phenomenon that is related to, and also difficult to clearly distinguish from, polysemy, namely what an expression can be used to denote via *coercion*. As a terminological note, *coercion* has also been characterised as *selectional polysemy*, in contrast to *inherent polysemy* or *logical polysemy* that we have been calling just *polysemy*. (See Pustejovsky, 1995, 2008.) The example in (40), for instance, could be taken to show that *book* has a sense that denotes an eventuality, namely that of reading or writing a book.

---

[14] This is similar to a test for lexical ambiguity proposed in Kripke (1977).
[15] We hedge with 'more likely' here, since it is not the case that all polysemies are reflected in even closely related languages. For instance, the verb *schwimmen* in German is polysemous between 'swim' and 'float', unlike in English.

(40)   Mary began the book.   (Pustejovsky, 1995)

However, one can see that *book* does not straightforwardly have an eventuality-denoting sense when we look at a wider range of modifiers, especially in out-of-the-blue contexts. For example, out-of-the-blue temporal modification, as we have in (41) is much less natural than the modifiers *thick* and *interesting*.

(41)   *War and Peace* is a thick/interesting/?six-month book.

Furthermore, the most natural reading for (42) is that Billie likes the contents of the book. Less salient is that Billie likes some physical aspect of the book (e.g. its heft). Without a much richer supporting context, however, the interpretation that Billie likes reading/writing the book is not obviously available.

(42)   Billie likes this book.

In richer contexts, examples such as (41) improve, however, suggesting that contextual support makes an eventuality reading of *book* more accessible (Sutton, 2022, p. 337, fn. 3). The following example is taken from the English Web 2020 (enTenTen20) corpus:[16]

(43)   He has actually set it up to be read in 40 days (no comparison though to that other 40 day book)

Such cases are considered to be instances of *coercion*, also called *selectional polysemy*, in contrast to cases of polysemy as described earlier, also called *inherent polysemy* (Pustejovsky, 2008, 2011).[17] Coercion is analysed as involving an implicit operation that shifts the meaning of an expression such as *book* into something denoting an event, where the application of this operation is licensed by a type mismatch. For example, in (40), *began* selects for an eventuality-denoting expression, and since *book* does not denote an eventuality, this prompts a type-shifting operation that coerces the in-context interpretation

---

[16] We make use of different corpora within the Ten-Ten family (Jakubíček et al., 2013). Examples were sourced using the SketchEngine tool (Kilgarriff et al., 2004). Most corpus examples in this section were first discussed in Sutton (2022).

[17] We surmise that further evidence for coercion over polysemy is the presence of underspecification that can be made explicit by filling in some extra content. For the case in hand, the eventuality-denoting interpretation of *a book* is underspecified between, say, READING a book and WRITING a book. Similarly, for other cases of coercion, such as mass-to-count coercion, we get a similar effect. For instance, absent further context, the coerced interpretation of *two white wines* leaves open whether it is two GLASSES OF wine, BOTTLES OF wine or KINDS OF wine and so on (see Sutton & Filip, 2021 for discussion). The same does not seem to be so for polysemous senses. Indeed, 'making explicit' the sense of *book* for these senses is marked: ?*an interesting book content*, ?*a thick book object*.

of *(the) book* into something that (also) denotes an eventuality (by inserting some implicit content such as READING *the book*).

In the context of MTTs, type coercions have been used in order to formulate a subtyping mechanism, called *coercive subtyping* (Luo, 1999, 2011). Coercive subtyping be seen as an abbreviation mechanism: A is a subtype of B ($A \leq B$) if there is a unique implicit coercion c from type A to type B and, if so, an object a of type A can be used in any context $\mathfrak{C}_B[\_]$ that expects an object of type B: $\mathfrak{C}_B[a]$ is legal (well-typed) and equal to $\mathfrak{C}_B[c(a)]$. Subtyping relations like the following can then be declared:

(44) $[\![human]\!] \leq [\![animal]\!]$

Now, the same mechanism can be used in a local rather than a global manner. For example, one might want to be able to capture the semantics of a sentence like "the ham sandwich" in a local context, as in:

(45) The ham sandwich is sitting at table 20. (Nunberg, 1979, p. 149)

The solution proposed by Luo (2011) is based on both the notion of coercive subtyping and the type-theoretic notion of context. As we have already mentioned in Section 2, a context in type theory is of the form

$x_1 : A_1, \ldots, x_n : A_n$

Now, the formal notion of context can be extended to include subtyping declarations as in Luo (2010). These *coercion contexts* are contexts with entries that might be in the form $A \leq_c B$, besides the $x : A$ form. The coercion context for our ham sandwich example could be something like the following:

(46) ..., *ham sandwich* $\leq$ *human*, ...

Note that the coercive subtyping mechanism is used here for cases that have been taken as distinct in the literature: (a) regular subtyping relations and (b) meaning transfers. The difference between the two under this view just lies in whether the subtyping declaration is considered global or local. In effect, this is close to Pustejovsky's inherent versus selectional polysemy distinction. In the first instance polysemy is global, that is, not affected by contextual relations, whereas in the latter case it is contextual. The mechanism used in MTTs is the same in both cases, namely coercive subtyping. The difference is the scope coercions take, that is, over the whole global context, or locally, over a specified local context. This topic is taken up in Gregoromichelaki et al.[18] There we argue

---

[18] Forthcoming (see n. 4 for details).

that for a more complete explanation of such phenomena we need to recruit incremental update mechanisms within the grammar, in particular a dynamic view of context updates.

Finally, let us briefly consider a phenomenon that is related to, and not necessarily even clearly separable from, polysemy, namely *underspecification*. To take an example from Recanati (2010) (originally discussed by Searle, 1980), the verb *cut* can be used to describe rather different actions, such as cutting grass versus cutting a cake. In fact, there are many different ways in which something can be cut; however, one can still be accused of not cutting something in the right way in context (e.g., by cutting the grass as you would a cake). An appealing idea is that the semantics of *cut* underspecifies whether cutting is, for instance, instantiated as the kind of horizontal mowing type of cutting or the vertical slicing type of cutting. A question that arises is whether this is connected to polysemy of the kind we have so far discussed.

Although we, once again, will not provide a clear-cut means of distinguishing these phenomena (not least in part because we doubt one can be given), one way of trying to tease these notions apart is with respect to whether we can think of different perspectives on what can be the same situation (polysemy) compared with differences between different situations each of which witnesses the relevant expression (underspecification). The case of *cut* exemplifies the latter. There can be many and various cutting situations that vary based upon what is being cut and the purposes of the individuals, but relative to a single situation, the action in question counts as a cutting eventuality or it does not, however it is actualised (unless, perhaps, it is a borderline case of a cutting). In contrast, an example of verbal polysemy is arguably *ausleihen* ('borrow', German) in (47), also attested in some British English dialects (48) for *borrow* in which the same verb can be used to describe both a borrowing and a lending eventuality:

(47) German
    a. Alex hat ein Buch von Bertha ausgeliehen.
       Alex AUX a book from Bertha borrow.PST_PTCPL
       'Alex borrowed a book from Bertha'
    b. Bertha hat Alex ein Buch ausgeliehen.
       Bertha AUX Alex a book borrow.PST_PTCPL
       'Bertha lent a book to Alex'

(48) British English, Lancashire dialect
    a. I borrowed a book from Billie.
    b. Billie borrowed me a book.
       'Billie lent me a book', natural data

Here, and unlike with *cut*, we may have one situation (i.e., one Fillmorean frame) which can be conceptualised in different ways: as a lending or as a borrowing. (In these cases, the intended sense can be communicated based upon direct–indirect object alternation.) Likewise, for nominal polysemy such as *lunch*, the different senses of *lunch* can be used to 'focus in on' different sides to one situation in which a food-eating event takes place: we can frame lunch as an event, as the food eaten or as both at once. Indeed, arguably, it is this feature of polysemy that makes copredication possible insofar as we can describe distinct, but interrelated parts of the same situation in different ways. This contrasts with a case of nominal underspecification such as vagueness. The meaning of *kitten* does not fully specify the age/maturity level at which a young cat ceases to be a kitten, but this is not a case of polysemy.

In summary, the multiple senses of polysemous expressions do not seem to have arisen as a result of the kind of accidental homonymy associated with lexical ambiguity. Polysemy is also distinguishable from coercion phenomena at least insofar as polysemous expressions lexically encode their different senses in a way that the interpretation of an expression as the result of coercion does not. Clear cases of polysemy are also potentially separable from classic cases of underspecification with respect to the satisfaction conditions of natural language expressions (used in context).

3.1.2 Copredication

One interesting feature of polysemous nouns is that one can use a single instance of the target expression to express more than one of its senses. In other words, polysemous expressions facilitate *copredication*. For instance, as noted earlier, *lunch* in English is polysemous between an eating event and the food consumed, and both of these senses can be expressed based on a single use of *lunch* as in (49). Furthermore, this pattern is attested in other languages in which the noun denoting lunch has these two senses, as we see for German in (50).

(49) Following a quick but delicious lunch, we were on the ferry back home [...][19]　　　　　　　　　　　　　　　　　　　　　　　　[enTenTen21]

(50) Ein absoluter Geheimtipp für das schnelle aber qualitativ
　　　a　absolute　secret.tip　for the fast　but　qualitatively
　　　hochwertige Mittagessen.
　　　high.value　lunch
　　　'An absolute insider's tip for a quick, but high-quality lunch'
　　　　　　　　　　　　　　　　　　　　　　　　　　　　[deTenTen20]

---

[19] This corpus example is similar, in the relevant respects, to a constructed example given in Asher and Pustejovsky (2006).

Furthermore, the naturalness of copredication gives us another means of separating polysemy from lexical ambiguity, since polysemous expressions usually license copredication across different senses, but lexically ambiguous nouns do not (Asher, 2011). For instance, the lexically ambiguous noun *party* gives rise to zeugmatic effects when we attempt to copredicate across its senses. In (51a), the intended reading is between the celebration and the travelling group, and the intended reading in (51b) is between the celebration and the political faction.

(51) a. ?The party went on until midnight and so left base-camp later than planned.
 b. ?The party went on until midnight and so elected their new leader later than planned.

Interestingly, coerced interpretations of expressions can license copredication across their coerced sense and their original senses, which suggests that coercion does not override the senses an expression has, but rather adds an extra sense in context. For example, (52) is an example of copredication across the informational and physical sense of *book* in addition to the coerced 'beginning to read' eventuality interpretation:

(52) Cal picked up and began an interesting book on morphology.

A further complexity of copredication is that for some more than two-ways polysemous expressions such as *statement* (38), while some combinations of senses support copredication (53a, 53b), others do not do so absent further contextual support (53c) (see also Ortega-Andrés & Vicente, 2019; Sutton, 2022 and references therein):[20]

(53) a. Alex's statement lasted 30 minutes and was not entirely true.
 b. Alex's statement is on the desk and is not entirely true.
 c. ?Alex's statement lasted 30 minutes and is on the desk.

In the next two sections, Sections 3.2 and 3.3, we outline two puzzles. The first puzzle is based on polysemy and copredication. We argue that it shows us that a semantic analysis of polysemy requires one to adopt a type theory that is richer than that standardly assumed as part of the simply-typed λ-calculus. The second puzzle is based on counting and copredication. We argue that this puzzle forces one to adopt a semantic theory that has a richer structure than that

---

[20] Examples similar to (53c) can be improved in context. For instance, suppose that all of the statements given at a trial were transcribed. Some stating events lasted less than 30 minutes; others were longer. In this case, one could say of the transcriptions, for instance, *The under-30-minute statements are on the desk.*

standardly assumed in formal semantic theories based on predicate modal logic and the simply-typed λ-calculus. The richness of structure and type theory are closely related, a matter we shall discuss later. In each section, we set out how these puzzles can be addressed via a more richly typed semantics and a more richly structured semantics, respectively.

3.2 The Polysemy and Copredication Puzzle and Richer Systems of Types

3.2.1 The Polysemy and Copredication Puzzle

Chomsky (2000) put forward an argument that the phenomena of polysemy and copredication force one to abandon externalist, truth-conditional semantics (see also Collins, 2017; Pietroski, 2003, among others, for discussion and reiteration). Collins (2017) argues as follows: Nouns such as *book* are polysemous, not lexically ambiguous. For example, *book* is polysemous between its informational contents and a physical object (that bears this content). However, not all uses of *book* evoke both senses, as we see in (54a) and (54b), but via copredication, both can be expressed, (54c).

(54)   Collins, 2017, p. 679

    a.   Bill memorised the book
    b.   Bill burnt the book
    c.   Bill memorised and (then) burnt the book

Collins (2017) claims that if nouns like *book* had an invariant, truth-conditional meaning between both the physical object sense and the informational contents sense (like a lexically ambiguous noun such as *party*), then cases of copredication like (54c) would be anomalous, contrary to fact. Therefore, nouns like *book* do not have an invariant, truth-conditional meaning.

Unpacking this argument, it contains an implicit premise that there are no alternatives between assigning an expression either one meaning, or the other, or otherwise two distinct meanings akin to a lexically ambiguous expression. This assumption may well hold for simply-typed formal languages, but, as we will show in Section 3.2.2, it does not hold for more richly typed semantic theories. At best, therefore, the argument shows that we cannot assign an 'invariant' meaning to polysemous expressions within a simply-typed semantics.[21] Canonical semantic theories in the Carnap-Montague-Lewis tradition assume that

---

[21] A separate issue is how much, if any, invariant meaning, in the traditional sense, should be assumed in the first place as opposed to an underspecified or intrinsically malleable interpretation.

the interpretation of a common noun is a function from possible worlds to an extension, where this extension is a set of entities. For instance, *book* might be analysed as in (55) where variable x is of type e (for entity), and variable w is of type s for possible worlds (if, following Gallin, 1975, a distinct type is assumed for possible worlds/world-time pairs), where, relative to a model, the interpretation of (55) is a function from worlds to entities to truth values.

(55) $book \mapsto \lambda w.\lambda x.BOOK_w(x)$

Now, the above argument from Collins can be reformulated as follows. Even if type e includes both physical entities and informational entities, if *book* refers to only one or the other in each use, we cannot explain cases of copredication. If, however, *book* applies to things, each of which is both a physical entity and an informational entity, then we cannot explain why *book* can be used to refer to one to the exclusion of the other.[22] Therefore, there is no set of things of type e that can be the extension of *book* in any world in which there are both physical books and informational books.

The situation is arguably worse if we assume, as is often at least implicitly done, that the domains of simple types are disjoint. Take as an example that the domains for eventualities and physical entities are disjoint. Upon this assumption, *lunch*, which is polysemous between an eventuality of type v and food of type e, denotes things belonging to one of two disjoint sets, one of type e and one of type v. This is problematic, however, since there is no means, within the simply-typed λ-calculus, of typing a variable that can be both of type e and of type v.[23]

To reiterate, the challenge is that a polysemous expression such as *book* can be used to refer to a physical thing, an informational entity and, via copredication, to both. As this reformulation of Collins' argument should make clear, it goes through only if there is no way to capture these data within one's semantic theory. Now, whereas we may grant this on the assumption that our semantic theory is restricted to being underpinned by a system of simple types, there is no reason why we should make this assumption. As we discuss in Section 3.2.2, there are a number of ways of treating polysemy and copredication within more richly typed frameworks. At best, therefore, the argument shows us only that we need to abandon (a particularly simple version of a) simply-typed semantics.

---

[22] An further option remains, since there could be three entities: the physical book, the informational contents and something which is, in some sense, both. As we shall discuss in Section 3.3.2, one way of taking this option is to have the physical book, the informational contents and their mereological sum (Gotham, 2014, 2017).

[23] As discussed in Asher (2011), this is an over-simplification, since if one allows product types, ⟦lunch⟧ could be typed $\langle s, \langle e \times v, t \rangle \rangle$. We discuss this option further in Section 3.2.2.

Types and the Structure of Meaning

In summary, the phenomena of polysemy and copredication are, genuinely, problematic for semantic theories based upon the simply-typed λ-calculus. However, far from entailing an abandonment of extensional, compositional semantics, analysing polysemy and copredication requires that we move beyond simply-typed semantics to something richer.

3.2.2 Richer Type Theories to Analyse Polysemy

A number of proposals for addressing polysemy and copredication have been made, all of which, in some way or another, adopt a type theory that is richer than that of the simply-typed λ-calculus. We discuss four of these approaches in turn. In each case, we will abstract over many of the details of specific theories in order to better elucidate the similarities and differences between different approaches. Our starting point will be to set out how each approach assumes an enrichment of a simple system of types.

In a system of simple types, there is at least one basic type and at least one type constructor. Typically (within a Gallin TY2 semantics), the set of basic types assumed is minimally $\{e, t, s\}$, but is often enriched with other basic types such as v (for eventualities) and/or d for degrees. The single type constructor that is normally assumed is one that constructs functional types.

(56) **Types.** (Carpenter, 1997, p. 40)
From a non-empty set **BasTyp** of basic types, the set **Typ** of types is the smallest set such that:

a. **BasTyp** ⊆ **Typ**
b. $\langle \sigma, \tau \rangle \in$ **Typ** if $\sigma, \tau \in$ **Typ** (functional types)

Dot-Types and Aspects

One enrichment of the simply-typed λ-calculus is Type Compositional Logic (TCL, Asher, 2011; Asher & Pustejovsky, 2006), which (in addition to extending the system of types in other ways) adds a dot-type constructor:[24]

(57) (56) and:
d. $\sigma \bullet \tau \in$ **Typ** if $\sigma, \tau \in$ **Typ** (dot-types)

The philosophical/ontological justification for dot-types is the idea that polysemous expressions refer to entities that have different *aspects*. For instance, the intuition is that *lunch* refers to something that has a food aspect and an

---

[24] The use of dot-types is not restricted to TCL, however. Modern Type Theory treatments of polysemy and copredication also employ dot-types. We will discuss MTT approaches in more detail in Section 3.3 when we discuss a copredication puzzle relating to counting and quantification.

eating-event aspect. Dot-types are introduced to model this intuition. For types *phys* and *ev* for physical entities and eventualities, respectively, *lunch* denotes entities of type *phys • ev*, that is, entities that have a physical entity aspect and an eventuality aspect. As stressed by Asher and Pustejovsky (2006), this is not meant to commit one to 'complex objects', only to complex types. However, this does at least prompt a metaphysical question. If *lunch* can be used to refer to *one* thing that can be conceptualised as either food or an event, is this one thing more ontologically or metaphysically complex than, say, a physical entity such as a chair?

The addition of a dot-type constructor already accounts at least for simple cases of polysemy and copredication (however, see the counting and copredication puzzle in Section 3.3). For instance, (55) for *book* can be updated to the following (where p is the type for physical object and i is the type for informational entity), that is, we get a property of entities, namely books, that have both a physical and an informational aspect:

(58) $book \mapsto \lambda w.\lambda x_{:p \bullet i}.BOOK_w(x)$

An Aside on Product Types

The product type constructor, the type for ordered tuples of entities, is often assumed implicitly or explicitly within a number of theories and frameworks.[25] Indeed, there does not seem to be consensus on whether a system of simple types should include a product type constructor or not. (Although the use of product types is only recently becoming more widespread in formal semantics, in other disciplines that use the simply-typed λ-calculus, and programming languages based upon it, the use of product types is completely standard.) Product types are defined in (59) and a product-type version of (58) is given in (60).

(59)   (Carpenter, 1997, p. 65). (56) and:
         d. $\langle \sigma \times \tau \rangle \in$ **Typ** if $\sigma, \tau \in$ **Typ**   (product types)

(60) $book \mapsto \lambda w.\lambda x_{:p \times i}.BOOK_w(x)$

Already in Pustejovsky (1995), product types are used as part of the analysis of dot-types, where, for instance, *book* is analysed (in part) as denoting entities of the product type $p \times i$, where these entities are related under the Formal Meaning component of the Generative Lexicon. An analysis of dot-types

---

[25] See, for instance, Carpenter, 1997; Rothstein, 2010; van Benthem, 1990, and even implicitly in Montague's IL in which the members of a domain of type $\langle s, a \rangle$ are functions from ordered pairs of $\langle w, t \rangle$ to entities of type a. Under Gallin's (1975) axiomatisation of IL, TY2, in which we also assume separate basic types t and w, these would be functions of type $\langle w \times t, a \rangle$.

can therefore be given by making use of product types and projection functions. For further background and discussion, see Pustejovsky (1995), chapter 7, especially with regard to sub-typing, as well as Asher (2011), section 5.2.2.

However, an analysis in terms of product types is rather less well suited as an implementation of *aspects*, since, properly speaking, common nouns such as *book* would denote not one thing that has different aspects but rather two things under some ordering. This later conception of how to treat polysemy, albeit framed in terms of situations that witness (i.e., contain) multiple entities of different types, is discussed later *Situation- and Frame-Theoretic Semantics* and shares some commonalities with Pustejovsky's (1995) original proposal.

Product types also reveal a clear way in which enriching the type theory and enriching the structure of, say, lexical entries within the semantic theory are highly interrelated. As we discuss more at length in Section 3.3, there are reasons to assume that the meanings of some expressions involve two sets of entities (the extension and something else). Such a bipartite approach to the lexicon can be encoded with product types. For instance, if the extension set of an expression is P and one also wants to make available some subset of P, Q, which also satisfies condition $\mathcal{R}$, this can be defined as in (61a) which would have the type in (61b):

(61)   a. $\lambda x. \exists Q. \langle P(x),\ \lambda y.Q(y) \wedge Q \subseteq P \wedge \mathcal{R}(Q) \rangle$

          b. $\langle e, \langle t \times \langle e, t \rangle \rangle \rangle$

Situation- and Frame-Theoretic Semantics

The final proposals we will consider are framed within TTR, a form of situation-theoretic semantics (see Section 2 for an introduction to TTR), and Barsalou-inspired 'Düsseldorf Frame' semantics. The latter uses attributes to model Pustejovskyan aspects in the Generative Lexicon. One TTR proposal adopts the intuitions behind aspects as modelled by dot-types, but employs predicates as type constructors and ptypes (types constructed from predicates) instead of dot-types (Cooper, 2011). The other TTR proposal treats polysemous expressions denoting situations that are constrained so as to witness multiple entities of different types (Sutton, 2022). Both TTR proposals make the same assumptions regarding an enrichment of the simple theory of types. While this amounts to a greater modification of the type theory compared to previous approaches, it can be pointed out that there are independent motivations behind these enrichments (as we have seen in Section 2 for the attitudes). See also Gregoromichelaki et al. where we argue that richer structures are also needed for modelling dialogue.[26] That is to say, unlike TCL, the enrichments to simple type theory assumed in TTR are not primarily introduced for the treatment of copredication and polysemy.

Aspects modelled with predicate types: Cooper (2011) points out that, given the system of types in TTR, one does not need a dot-type constructor to be able to represent aspects. Cooper's analysis of *lunch* is given in (62) in which the dependent predicate type lunch_ev_fd($r.x, e, f$) should be understood to be the type of situation in which the entity labelled by x in r has two aspects, that of being f of type *food* and that of being e of type *event*.

(62) $\quad lunch \mapsto \lambda r: \begin{bmatrix} x:Ind \end{bmatrix} . \begin{bmatrix} f & : & food \\ e & : & event \\ c_{lunch} & : & lunch\_ev\_fd(r.x, e, f) \end{bmatrix}$

This account makes use of the fact that, in TTR, predicates are type constructors (see also Section 1.4 about dependent types). For instance, the predicate 'cat' can be used to construct any of many ptypes (the witnesses of which are situations) such as cat(felix), cat(garfield) and cat(tibbles). This predicates-as-type-constructors approach is then expressive enough to articulate the type of situation in which some entity has a food aspect and an event aspect.

Multiple participant situations: Sutton (2022) takes a different approach which departs from the Pustejovskyan/Asherian view that polysemous items denote single entities with different aspects. Instead, the main difference between polysemous and non-polysemous expressions is characterised in terms of how they constrain the situations they denote, specifically as part of the type restrictor on the record argument variable r. Sutton's analysis of *lunch* is given in (63). The idea is that, unlike a non-polysemous noun denoting, for instance, a situation that witnesses a physical entity of type *Ind*, a polysemous expression denotes a situation that is lexically constrained to witness at least two entities, possibly of different types.[27] This idea is exemplified in (63), in which the situations denoted by *lunch* are constrained to witness at least some event and some individual, where the resulting record type constrains the event to be a lunch-eating event and the individual to be the food.

(63) $\quad lunch \mapsto \lambda r: \begin{bmatrix} x:Ind \\ e:Ev \end{bmatrix} . \begin{bmatrix} c_{food} & : & food(r.x) \\ c_{eat} & : & eat\_lunch(r.e) \\ c_{pat} & : & patient(r.x, r.e) \end{bmatrix}$

---

[26] Forthcoming (see n. 4 for details).
[27] Sutton does not use type *Ind*; however, the basis for this is orthogonal to the issues we discuss here, and so, for consistency of presentation, we use *Ind*.

This makes Sutton's analysis closer to the one we outlined earlier based upon product types: Polysemous expressions, in a sense, denote multiplicities of things (e.g., an event and a physical entity), but these things are related in a certain way. Indeed, motivated by constraints on copredication such as in (53), Sutton also argues that polysemous common nouns specify how these entities are related (if at all). For instance, for lunches, the food is the patient (more specifically, the incremental theme (Dowty, 1991; Krifka, 1989)) of the eating event. Concretely, Sutton hypothesises that a precondition of felicitous copredication is that there is a lexically or contextually provided relation between the entities over which copredication occurs. For instance, the infelicity of (53c) compared to (53a) and (53b) is explained because there is no direct relation between a physical written statement and a spoken stating event, although there is a relation between the event and the information conveyed and a relation between the written artefact and the information it contains, namely, in both cases, a contents relation. For a related idea, albeit from a more psychologically, as opposed to semantically, oriented perspective, see Ortega-Andrés and Vicente (2019).

Düsseldorf-Style Frame Semantics

Working within a frame theory inspired by the work of Barsalou (e.g., Barsalou, 1992), Babonnaud, Kallmeyer and Osswald (2016) and Kallmeyer and Osswald (2017) reinterpret Pustejovskyan aspects as attributes in a frame. For *book*, the attribute CONTENT links the physical book to the content. This attribute therefore plays the role of the Formal Meaning component in the lexical entry for *book* in Pustejovsky's (1995) Generative Lexicon account, which is a relation $hold(x,y)$ with x the informational contents of the book and y the physical book.

(64)

All attributes (edges in a graph) are functional (for any argument, they return one value) (see, e.g., Löbner, 2015; Petersen, 2015). Nodes are typed, so the values of the left- and right-hand nodes in (64) must be of type *book* and *information*, respectively.

Frames, even for polysemous nouns, have one central node (indicated by the double ring) determining the reference of the concept, for example the physical book for *book*. Therefore, Babonnaud, Kallmeyer and Osswald assume that every polysemous item has a 'primary' reference dictated by what one takes to be the central node. This amounts to the claim that, for instance, the primary or default reference for *book* is the physical book.[28] On this view, uses of *book* to denote informational entities are better seen as a type of coercion (shifting the central node of the frame), where such coercions are restricted by, for example, what is the *Formal* Meaning component of the Generative Lexicon.

The Polysemy Puzzle: Interim Summary

We began this section with a version of an argument from polysemy that seeks to conclude that we must reject externalist and/or truth-conditional semantics. However, we have argued that the only conclusion that should be drawn from the challenges of polysemy is that it requires a semantic theory based upon something richer than the simply-typed λ-calculus. Although not made explicit in the earlier examples, almost all the more richly typed approaches to polysemy also make use of additional structure in lexical representations. In Section 3.3, we turn to the puzzle of counting and copredication that, we argue, necessitates this extra structure in addition to the richer type theory required for a treatment of polysemy. Before this, however, we briefly outline some alternative responses to the Chomskyan challenge.

3.2.3 Simply-Typed Alternatives

Mereologically Complex Entities

An alternative to aspects and dot-types, proposed by Gotham (2014, 2017, 2021), is to assume that, instead of entities with different aspects, we have entities with a mereologically complex constitution. The enrichment of simply-typed semantics with Classical Extensional Mereology (CEM) has been proposed to account for a broad range of phenomena including plurality, collectivity and distributivity, countability classes, aspect, and partitive constructions (see, among many others, Bach, 1986; Champollion, 2017; Chierchia, 1998; Filip, 1993/1999; Landman, 1991; Link, 1983). Classical Extensional Mereology is the formal theory of parts and sums. For an overview of the development of and variations within CEM, see, for instance, Champollion and Krifka (2016) and references therein.

Although there are different ways of defining the primitives in CEM, Krifka (1986, 1989) provides one way of doing so in which we take sum as a basic operation and define part-hood in terms of it. The sum operation for type τ, $\sqcup_\tau$, is a complete, commutative, idempotent and associative operation between two

---

[28] In their latest work, Chen, Kallmeyer and Osswald (2022) incorporate dot-types into their analysis.

entities of type τ (Krifka, 1989, p. 77) (where there is no risk of confusion, we drop typing subscripts hereon).

(65)   a. $\forall x \forall y [(\exists P \exists P'[P(x) \wedge P'(y)]) \rightarrow \exists z[x \sqcup y = z]]$ (completeness)
       b. $\forall x \forall y [x \sqcup y = y \sqcup x]$ (commutativity)
       c. $\forall x \forall y [x \sqcup x = x]$ (idempotency)
       d. $\forall x \forall y \forall z [(x \sqcup y) \sqcup z = x \sqcup (y \sqcup z)]$ (associativity)

In words, for any two entities, there is some sum of them that exists (65a), the sum of two entities a and b is identical to the sum of b and a (65b), the sum of any entity with itself is identical to that entity (65c) and the sum operation is not sensitive to the order in which it is applied (65d). However, importantly, it is not the case that for any sum there is a simple, non-conjunctive natural language predicate that denotes this sum, even if there are such natural language predicates that denote the entities that are parts of the sum. For example, there may be sums of single cats and single planets, but no simple (non-conjunctive) natural language expression that denotes the sums of cats and planets. That is to say, in the words of Lewis (1991), sum formation is *ontologically innocent*.

In simple terms, the incorporation of CEM into a classical formal semantics amounts to enriching the domain (usually of type e and, for verbal semantics, type v) so that it not only contains (single) entities but also contains all of the possible sums thereof. Thus, the domain is structured as a Boolean semi-lattice closed under sum (minus the bottom element). From sum, we can define relations such as part-hood $\sqsubseteq$ and proper part-hood $\sqsubset$ (Krifka, 1989).

(66)   a. $\forall x \forall y [x \sqsubseteq y \leftrightarrow x \sqcup y = y]$ (part)
       b. $\forall x \forall y [x \sqsubset y \leftrightarrow x \sqsubseteq y \wedge x \neq y]$ (proper part)

The main idea behind Gotham's approach is that polysemous expressions denote material sum entities, where the relata of the sum may be of different sorts of things, for example physical entities or informational entities. Gotham treats all of these entities as being of type e. Therefore, the information contained in a book is an entity, just like the physical book. In this sense, Gotham posits that the denotations of polysemous nouns are entities that have a complex structure: books are sums of informational things and physical things.

However, there are arguably good reasons not to want to commit to, for example, informational contents being the same type as physical objects. For instance, take a piece of paper with a declarative sentence written upon it. If propositions are the interpretations of declarative sentences and are of type $\langle s, t \rangle$, then one seemingly has to commit to there being both the (propositional) information that the sentence on the paper expresses as well as a distinct material part of the piece of paper that is its informational contents.

Based upon such considerations, this approach to polysemy could be implemented in a richer type theory by slightly modulating standard assumptions relating to CEM and adding an additional type constructor. In relation to type-specific mereological operations (e.g., $\sqcup_e$, $\sqcup_v$, etc.), one could assume that sums can be formed between entities of different types. We could therefore have an entity that is the sum of a physical book and an informational book. The use of such sum entities prompts the question as to their type, which could be given via addition of a sum type constructor:

(67)   (56) and:

       d. $\sigma \sqcup \tau \in$ **Typ** if $\sigma, \tau \in$ **Typ**   (sum types)

where, if an entity $a \sqcup b$ is the sum of $a : \tau$ and $b : \sigma$, then $a \sqcup b : \tau \sqcup \sigma$. We return to some of the nuances of Gotham's approach when discussing the copredication puzzle in Section 3.3.

Property Inheritance and a Denial of Polysemy

Although in most, if not all, of the semantics literature it is taken as uncontroversial that expressions such as *lunch* and *book* are polysemous, a recent reaction to the grounds for this assumption has come from the philosophical metaphysics literature (Liebesman & Magidor, 2017, 2019). Let us first examine some of the evidence for polysemy in an expression. Primarily, aside from introspective intuitions, the evidence for whether an expression has a particular kind of sense comes from the modifiers, verb phrases and so on that are straightforwardly compatible with it. As we saw earlier for *book* in (41), for example, since in *interesting book*, 'interesting' can be used to describe the contents of a book, and since 'thick' in *thick book* can be used to describe the physical dimensions of the book, then we have some reason to believe that *book* can denote a physical thing or its informational contents. Compare, for instance, the following contrasts which indicate that there are some modifiers that select for physical entities or objects and are incompatible as modifications for events (*thick/thin/heavy/red*), others which select for some kind of informational context and cannot modify events (*misleading/mostly true*) and others which can also be used to describe events (*interesting*) (because, for instance, the outcome is interesting).

(68)   a.   thick/thin/heavy/red book/object
            b.   ?thick/thin/heavy/red party/event

(69) a. interesting/misleading/mostly true book/piece of information
      b. interesting/?misleading/?mostly true party/event

In response to such considerations, Liebesman and Magidor (2017) (L&M) argue that these data do not necessarily reveal the nature of the referents of nouns like *book*, since properties can be inherited via association relations. For instance, since physical books normally have informational contents, one can predicate of physical books descriptions of the information they contain. The intuition is that sentences such as the one in (70) do not force us to explain how we can copredicate over different sorts of entities, since this sentence can straightforwardly be about physical books described as interesting based on an inheritance of the properties of their contents.

(70) Three interesting books are on the shelf.

Without going into the merits or otherwise of this view of property inheritance, it is important to point out that accepting it has consequences for semantic theory, contrary to what L&M seem to suppose: 'By contrast, we argue that accounting for copredication requires no revisionary semantics or metaphysics, and that copredication is perfectly compatible with standard referential semantics' (Liebesman & Magidor, 2017, p. 132). Let us assume, as L&M seem to do, along with the account of property inheritance, that our semantic theory is based upon the simply-typed λ-calculus, such that, for instance, there are disjoint sets of physical books and informational books (p. 137), and that *book* denotes both physical books and informational books.[29] Based on these assumptions, one option for giving a semantics for *book* within a simply-typed semantic theory is a simply-typed system with only one basic type (a mono-typed system), possibly with the addition of *sorts*.

As we have seen, assuming the simply-typed λ-calculus, we cannot treat physical books and informational books as being of different types, since this necessitates, minimally, a type constructor other than functional types to accommodate the polysemy data, contrary to L&M's assumption. Therefore, instead, we could treat informational books and physical books as being entities of the same type. For instance, both could be of type τ, for some type τ. An advantage of this strategy would be that it would allow predicates such as $BOOK_w$ to be typed as $\langle \tau, t \rangle$, which would seem to be in line with L&M's claim that their view requires no revision of semantic theory and would allow *book* to apply to either physical or informational books.

---

[29] '[W]e'll argue that "book" has a single sense and it designates both informational and physical books' (Liebesman & Magidor, 2017, p. 132).

However, when we look beyond *book* to all polysemous expressions, we find nouns that are polysemous, for example, between eventualities and physical entities (*lunch*), between propositional complements, eventualities and physical entities (*statement*) and between institutions and physical entities (*newspaper*). For consistency, the type of each and any entity should also be reduced to type τ.[30]

The effect of this is that it starts to make less compelling the case for also assuming other types (such as t and v), since the roles of these types would be taken on by type τ. While for *book* it might be plausible to assume a subtype of τ for informational entities, such that these entities stand in relation to some propositional contents, and thereby retain the need for complex types such as $\langle s,t \rangle$, such a strategy is less compelling for, say, the contents of propositional attitudes that can be denoted by nouns such as *statement* and *belief*, and it is hard to see how this strategy might be extended to eventuality-denoting expressions. Arguably, then, the result would be a collapse of the type system into one with a single basic type:

(71) From a SINGLETON set **BasTyp** of basic types, the set **Typ** of types is the smallest set such that:
    a. **BasTyp** ⊆ **Typ**
    b. $\langle \sigma, \tau \rangle \in$ **Typ** if $\sigma, \tau \in$ **Typ**   (functional types)

That is, for some one basic type τ, members of the set **Typ** would include τ, $\langle \tau, \tau \rangle$, $\langle \langle \tau, \tau \rangle, \tau \rangle$ and $\langle \tau, \langle \tau, \tau \rangle \rangle$ and so on. There have been proposals for such a single basic type semantics (Liefke, 2014; Liefke & Werning, 2018; Partee, 2007), which include arguments for why, at least, DPs (determiner phrases) and CPs (complementizer phrases) should share a type. There has also been some limited discussion of why a richer type theory is preferable over one with a single basic type (Rett, 2022). Also, somewhat intermediary positions are available. For instance, *property theory* as presented in Chierchia and Turner (1988) adopts a monotype system based on a general entity type and distinguishes between sorts of e (basic individuals, nominalised functions and information units). (For a discussion of sorts, see Kohlhase, 1992, 1994.)

Düsseldorf Frame Theory can be understood as assuming a sorted domain in which, for example, mammals are a sort of entity and cats are a sort of mammal and so on. And some selectional restrictions can be specified in terms of sorts. The question then becomes whether one wants to allow for combinations of

---

[30] As observed by Sutton (2022), an alternative formalisation of L&M's theory that would mean conceding that this view does, after all, necessitate 'revisionary semantics' is to implement it with join types. For instance, *lunch* would denote entities that are of type e or v.

sorts via something like a complex sort constructor (e.g., meet sorts, join sorts or dependent sorts), whereupon sorts would start to look increasingly like types.

In summary, a surprising outcome of our discussion of polysemy seems to be that we need either, minimally, to extend our system of type constructors or to put constraints on our set of basic types. In the latter case, we could not allow for eventualities and physical entities to be of different type, or possibly we could even collapse the set of basic types down to a singleton (depending on whether one is willing to countenance, say, differing types for propositions and the contents of stating events and beliefs etc.).

3.3 The Counting and Copredication Puzzle and Richer Semantic Structures

3.3.1 The Counting and Copredication Puzzle

The second puzzle arises when we look at polysemous expressions in the wider context of quantificational DPs and numeral constructions.[31] Without further restrictions, the following sentences are underspecified with respect to what kinds of entities are being quantified over:

(72)   a.   The spokesperson gave two statements to the press.
           b.   The spokesperson gave every statement to the press.

In (72a), for instance, it could be that the spokesperson was the agent of two statement events with the same informational content (e.g., to different groups of journalists at different times). Or, it could be that the informational content differed in each case. Alternatively still, the spokesperson could have given, as part of one event, statements on behalf of two people.[32] Needless to say, in every case there has to be (at least) two of something that can be individuated to make the sentence true. Similar points can be made with respect to (72b).

However, an enrichment of the linguistic (or also non-linguistic) context can restrict these readings.

(73)   a.   The spokesperson gave two five-minute statements to the press.
           b.   The spokesperson gave two misleading statements to the press.
           c.   The spokesperson gave two misleading, five-minute statements to the press.

---

[31] Here, we treat numeral-noun constructions as instances of adjectival modification; however, one could also treat them as generalised quantifiers (Barwise & Cooper, 1981).

[32] This could even be done within a single sentence, for example 'I have two statements to make: while X regrets the company's actions, Y maintains that the company behaved in good faith.'

The use of the modifier *five-minute* in (73a) seemingly makes the one-event – two-contents reading less plausible (or at least less salient). The use of the modifier *misleading* in (73b) likewise seemingly makes the two-events – one-content reading less plausible and/or salient. A combination of these modifiers in (73c) gives us only what Gotham (2017) dubs the 'double-distinctness' reading, that is, the reading on which there are both distinct events and distinct contents. The challenge for an account of copredication is how to predict these restrictions.[33]

Although there has been an awareness of some of the complexities of the interactions between numerals and quantifiers with co-predication (e.g., Asher, 2011), this puzzle was made more acute since Gotham (2014), in which it was shown that TCL approaches do not predict the double-distinctness reading for sentences such as *John picked up and mastered three books*. The reactions to this puzzle from those working within theories that assume a richer type system than the simply-typed λ-calculus, in addition to Gotham's own, interestingly converge on a similar conclusion, namely, that the semantics of common nouns and noun phrases requires some extra structure, specifically, something that tracks the individuation conditions of these expressions that, furthermore, can be updated in context.

In Section 3.3.2, we present two such approaches, Gotham's (2014) mereological approach and Chatzikyriakidis and Luo's (2018, 2020) approach of dot-types with identity criteria. In Section 3.3.3, we discuss reactions to this copredication puzzle that propose more pragmatic solutions, and also draw parallels between nominal semantics enriched with identity criteria, and the independently arrived-at proposal in the literature on countability that the semantics of count and mass nouns also requires a more richly structured semantic representation than is canonically assumed, namely, a field to track the individuation criteria of common nouns (i.e., what counts as 'one').

3.3.2 Richer Representations to Analyse Counting and Copredication

Mereological Semantics with Individuation Relations

Gotham has managed to provide a compositional account of copredication that derives the correct Individuation Criteria (ICs) in the cases where double distinctness is needed (Gotham, 2014, 2017). This is the first account to our

---

[33] An open issue is how strictly double-distinctness readings are enforced. For instance, the following seems to have a true reading:

(i) The spokesperson gave two identical misleading, five-minute statements to the press.

We return to this issue in Section 3.3.3.

knowledge that explicitly and successfully dealt with this problem. The main features of Gotham's account are as follows:

- Both complex and plural objects exist.
  - Complex objects are denoted with the + operator and plural objects with the ⊕ operator (assuming a join semilattice à la Link (1983)).
  - Any property that holds of p holds of $p + i$, and likewise any property that holds of i also holds of $p + i$.
- Lexical entries for common nouns and verbs are more complex than is traditionally assumed in Montague Grammar, in that they further specify a distinctness criterion.
- Different objects have different ICs (individuation relations in Gotham's terminology). They are two-place predicates of the following form:
  - PHYS = $\lambda x, y.phys\text{-}equiv(x)(y)$
  - INFO = $\lambda x, y.info\text{-}equiv(x)(y)$
- A non-compressibility statement denoting that no two members of a plurality stand in a relation R is introduced. This ensures that members of the plurality do not bear an R relation to each other (see Gotham (2014) for the formal definition of compressibility).
- A further assumption is that verbs also somehow point to the ICs that have to be used.
- Lastly, an operator, called Ω, is used for choosing the ICs for each argument.[34]

Some notes on the Ω operator are in place. Common nouns according to Gotham are not just plain predicates anymore. The type of common nouns like 'book' have the type $e \rightarrow (t \times ((e \rightarrow \mathbf{R}) \rightarrow t))$, abbreviated to $e \rightarrow T$. The second projection p_2 is a set of functions that map the type e argument to a relation of type $e \rightarrow R$, where $R \sqsubseteq R_{cn}$, and where R_{cn} is taken to be the individuation relation given by the noun or the predicate. For example, the lexical entry for *book* is now as follows (where $*P$ means that the predicate P is a set of pluralities):

(74) $books = \lambda y: e.\langle *book(y), \lambda f: e \rightarrow R.f(y) \sqsubseteq (\text{PHYS} \sqcup \text{INFO})\rangle$

Assuming such an entry for a common noun, the function Ω computes the least upper bound of the set of relations R. For *books* this is (PHYS⊔INFO), for *master* it is (INFO) and so on. Computing the semantics of 'John picked up and mastered three books' gives the following result:

---

[34] See Gotham (2014) for the formal definition.

(75) $\langle \exists x(|x \geq 3| \wedge {}^*book(x) \wedge {}^*pick\text{-}up(j')(x) \wedge {}^*master(j')(x) \wedge \neg(\text{PHYS} \sqcup \text{INFO})$
$(comp(x)), \lambda h: e \rightarrow R. \exists u({}^*book(u) \wedge h(u) \sqsubseteq (\text{PHYS} \sqcup \text{INFO}) \wedge h(j') \sqsubseteq$
$(\text{ANI})\rangle$

To put this into words: the formula talks of a plurality of three objects that are books, that are all picked up and mastered and that are neither informationally nor physically compressible (thus distinct). The second projection just gives the ICs for the arguments, PHYS ⊔ INFO for the object and ANI for the subject (animate). These are the correct ICs for the double-distinctness cases.

Modern Type Theory and Dot-Types with Identity Criteria

Dot-types and individuation have been dealt with using MTT semantics. In particular, Chatzikyriakidis and Luo (2015a, 2018, 2020) discuss the issue of individuation within a setting where dot-types are formalised as a complex type with two components, following earlier work by Luo (2011) and Xue and Luo (2012). In Chatzikyriakidis and Luo (2015a), the authors do not explicitly assume ICs, whereas in Chatzikyriakidis and Luo (2018, 2020) they introduce ICs for common nouns. Let us start with the account of dot-types without ICs.

Consider this copredication example (76):

(76)   John picked up and mastered the book.

Assume that *Phy* and *Info* are the types of physical and informational objects, respectively. Further assume that the interpretations of *pick up* and *master* have the following types:

$$pick\ up : Human \rightarrow Phy \rightarrow Prop$$
$$master : Human \rightarrow Info \rightarrow Prop$$

In (76), *pick up* and *master* are applied in coordination to *the book*. For this coordination to be licensed, the two verbs must be of the same type. The introduction of dot-types make this possible.

Informally, *Phy* • *Info* is the dot-type satisfying the following property: it is a subtype of both *Phy* and *Info*. The physical and informational aspect of *book* can be captured by assuming that *Book* is a subtype of *Phy* • *Info*:

$$Book \leq Phy \bullet Info \leq Phy$$
$$Book \leq Phy \bullet Info \leq Info$$

By contravariance of subtyping for function types, we have:

$$pick\ up : Human \rightarrow Phy \rightarrow Prop$$
$$\leq Human \rightarrow Phy \bullet Info \rightarrow Prop$$
$$\leq Human \rightarrow Book \rightarrow Prop$$

$$\text{master} : \text{Human} \to \text{Info} \to \text{Prop}$$
$$\leq \text{Human} \to \text{Phy} \bullet \text{Info} \to \text{Prop}$$
$$\leq \text{Human} \to \text{Book} \to \text{Prop}$$

In other words, *pick up* and *master* are both of type $\text{Human} \to \text{Book} \to \text{Prop}$ and, therefore, the coordination in (76) and its interpretation can proceed straightforwardly as intended.

This is the standard use of dot-types, where CNs are viewed as types and no ICs are assumed, at least explicitly. In Chatzikyriakidis and Luo (2015a), the authors claim that this is enough to solve the counting problem. However, in order to do so, they state axioms for equality under subtyping. They note (c stands for a coercive subtyping relation): 'In general, when $X <_c Y$, we do not have $x \neq_X y \implies (x \neq_Y y)$ unless c is injective. For the atomic types like *Book* and PHY, the equality on a subtype coincides with that of the supertype and so we can axiomatically assume this' (Chatzikyriakidis and Luo, 2015a, p. 45).

However, as Gotham (personal communication) pointed out, doing so overgenerates as it also predicts the following to be derived, where the ICs of physical objects and informational objects seem to be conflated:[35]

(77)   John picked up three books and John mastered every book $\Rightarrow$ John mastered three books.

In Chatzikyriakidis and Luo (2018, 2020) the authors refine their approach by proposing that CNs are setoids, that is, pairs where the first projection is their CN type and the second projection defines an equivalence relation on that type (the type's IC):

(78) $(A, =)$, where A is a type and $=: A \to A \to \text{Prop}$ is an equivalence relation over A.

In this setting, the type for humans will be defined as follows:

(79) $[human] = (\text{Human}, =_h)$, where $=_h : \text{Human} \to \text{Human} \to \text{Prop}$ is the equivalence relation that represents the identity criterion for humans (CNs-as-setoids view)

Moving to dot-types, the following two setoids are proposed for the two senses of *book*:[36]

---

[35] The fact that there are three distinct physical books does not imply that there are three distinct info books.
[36] Setoids will be denoted with small capitals.

(80)   BOOK$_1$ = (Book, =$_p$)

(81)   BOOK$_2$ = (Book, =$_i$)

The following definition is then proposed for the numerical quantifier *three*:[37]

(82)   [THREE] Let A be a type, B = (B, κ_B) a pre-setoid such that $A \leq B$, and $P: B \rightarrow Prop$:

$$\text{THREE}(A, \text{B}, P) = \exists x, y, z : A.D[\text{B}](x,y,z) \wedge P(x) \wedge P(y) \wedge P(z),$$

where $D[\text{B}](x,y,z) = \neg \kappa_B(x,y) \wedge \neg \kappa_B(y,z) \wedge \neg \kappa_B(x,z)$.

With this in place, distinctness can be captured:[38]

(83)   THREE(*Book, Phy • Info, pm(j)*)

(84) $\exists x, y, z: Book.D[Phy](x,y,z) \wedge D[Info](x,y,z) \wedge pm(j,x) \wedge pm(j,y) \wedge pm(j,z)$

The above account is quite elaborate and showcases the complexity of the problem. The bottom line is that if one wants to solve the issue of counting in co-predication, expressive machinery needs to be used, machinery that is not afforded by a standard Montagovian setting, at least in some straightforward sense.

The Counting and Copredication Puzzle: Summary

We argued in Section 3.2 that the polysemy and copredication puzzle provides a compelling reason to adopt a type theory richer than that of the simply-typed λ-calculus and, as such, is one motivation for adding structure to semantics. In this section, we have provided reasons for the claim that the counting and copredication puzzle also requires additional structure in semantics, namely, that expressions such as common nouns carry information about their possible ICs that can be updated and modified in context. Without such extra information, it is not clear how double-distinctness readings can be captured. To end this section, we will now draw parallels between this conclusion and work done on the semantics of the count/mass distinction, and additionally briefly discuss whether the solution to the counting and copredication puzzle should be treated more as a pragmatic phenomenon.

---

[37] Note that the definition for three involves a pre-setoid as the second argument B = (B, κ_B). A pre-setoid is a weaker version of the equivalence relation where transitivity does not hold. The dot-type is not necessarily a setoid, even if both its components are. However, it is a pre-setoid in case A and B are pre-setoids (in essence a setoid is also a pre-setoid, i.e., a setoid where transitivity does not hold). Given that the numeric quantifier will need to be applied to a dot-type in some cases, a pre-setoid is needed in the definition, instead of a setoid.

[38] We use the shorthand *pm(x)* to denote the conjunction *picked_up(x)* ∧ *mastered(x)*.

3.3.3 Other Reactions to the Puzzle and Connections with Countability
Convergence on an Idea: Polysemy and Countability

As we have argued in Section 3.3.2, a semantic solution to the counting and copredication puzzle requires keeping track not only of what (types of thing) an expression can be used to apply to but also of its ICs (which can be dynamically updated in context). Fascinatingly, a similar idea has emerged within the literature on the count–mass distinction based on completely independent data.

One puzzling feature of the count–mass (alternatively count–non-count) distinction in natural languages which have morphosyntactic bases for such categories is that this distinction does not align perfectly with the notional object–substance distinction (an observation that goes back at least as far as Quine, 1960, but has received more attention in recent decades, e.g., Barner & Snedeker, 2005; Chierchia, 1998; Landman, 2011, among many others). This provides a puzzle dubbed by Sutton and Filip (P. R. Sutton and H. Filip, Objects and the grammar of countability, Oxford University Press, forthcoming) *the co-extensionality puzzle*. In simple terms, this puzzle arises because there are mass nouns in some languages that are prima facie co-extensional (in fact prima facie co-intensional) with plural count nouns in others. For instance, *jewellery* in English is a mass noun (an *object mass noun*) which seems to mean exactly the same as the plural count noun *koru-t* ('jewellery item-s') in Finnish. This creates a puzzle for anyone who thinks (a) that countability distinctions are grounded in semantic (e.g., mereological or mereotopological) properties, and are not just, say, uninterpreted syntactic features; and (b) that the semantics of such expressions in a compositional semantics can be given in terms of a single set (or a function from worlds/situations to sets). Namely, if, relative to each world/situation, *jewellery* can be used to denote exactly the same entities as *koru-t*, we seem to have no basis for distinguishing these two in terms of countability.

There have been two main types of reactions to this puzzle. One denies the co-intensionality premise (i.e., that count-mass pairs like *koru-t* ('jewellery item-s', Finnish) and *jewellery* are co-intensional) (Chierchia, 2010, 2015); the other enriches the lexical entry of common nouns with a second set, the (*counting*) *base* set (Landman, 2011, 2016; Sutton & Filip, 2016, among others). To give a toy example, suppose that, in a situation, there are three items of jewellery a, b, c. On the first view, while *koru-t* ('jewellery item-s', Finnish) has an extension $\{a, b, c, a \sqcup b, a \sqcup c, b \sqcup c, a \sqcup b \sqcup c\}$ (a, b, c and all the mereological sums thereof), it is denied that the mass noun *jewellery* does so. Instead, in Chierchia's approach, *jewellery*, in this situation, would denote the singleton set $\{a \sqcup b \sqcup c\}$. On the second view, one can accept the co-intensionality premise, but instead claim that common nouns keep a record of a second set/individuation schema of what it is we can count. So, for *koru-t* ('jewellery.item-s', Finnish) this would be $\{a, b, c\}$, a set of the single items of jewellery, and for *jewellery*, $\{a, b, c, a \sqcup b, a \sqcup c, b \sqcup c, a \sqcup b \sqcup c\}$. The count–mass distinction is then characterisable in terms of properties of these second sets, for instance whether or not they are disjoint (pairwise non-overlapping) or quantized (have no members in proper part relations). Crucially, this second approach requires one to enrich the structure of the lexicon of common nouns such that these sets can be accessed by grammatical operations (e.g., to be the restrictor of a distributive determiner), for instance as functions to an entity with a product type (common nouns would be of type $\langle s, \langle e, \langle t \times \langle e, t \rangle \rangle \rangle \rangle$, Sutton & Filip, 2020) or to a frame, such as a TTR record type (Sutton & Filip, 2017). Interestingly, this second approach chimes well with the strategy for dealing with the counting and copredication puzzle, where a second set/type/individuation criterion is also required, suggesting some independent support for this idea.

A Pragmatic Phenomenon?

Liebesman and Magidor (2017) propose the following example and suggest that the sentence in (A) (their example (60), p. 155) has a reading on which the three books must each be physically distinct, but could have the same informational contents.

> Imagine that a certain library has a project of dusting each of its (physical) books. Moreover, since the informative books are much more popular among readers than the uninformative ones, they decide to start the project by dusting all the informative (physical) books in the library. …

> (A)   Three informative books are heavy, so take extra care as you're pulling them down from the shelf for dusting.

In response, Gotham (2021, s. 6.4) points out that this example can be explained away in terms of loose talk and slack regulation by contrasting the first clause of (A) with *Three different informative books are heavy*, which he claims once again enforces the double-distinctness reading. As such, the former could be considered an example of loose talk in which informational distinctness can be ignored if this does not clash with the goals of the agents doing the dusting (which is to distinguish only the heavy or the non-heavy books from the books that are informative).

The theoretical choice, therefore, seems to be whether to enforce double-distinctness readings and explain away possible counter-examples in terms of, for example, loose talk (Gotham, 2021), or else explain why, in many cases, the double-distinctness reading seems to be the only one available. In either case, there seems to be a reason for adding structure to semantics, since, in either case, the linguistic or extra-linguistic context seems to affect how we individuate polysemous expressions, even if the entities these expressions denote do not vary across the same contexts. For an intermediary position that assumes that modifiers like *informative* underspecify the ICs of the nouns they compose with, and that double-distinctness readings can be derived pragmatically, see the proposal, formulated in TTR, in Sutton (2024).

3.4 Summary

In this section we have discussed two interrelated puzzles: the polysemy and copredication puzzle, and the counting and copredication puzzle. The first of these puzzles is that expressions can carry multiple interrelated senses that can be expressed based upon a single antecedent (even with prima facie jointly inconsistent modifiers). Although this puzzle has been argued to show the futility of model-theoretic approaches to semantics, we have shown, on the contrary, that it merely shows us that a semantics based upon the simply-typed λ-calculus is untenable in the light of these data. The second puzzle that we have discussed is derived from the evidence that the use of quantifiers and numeral expressions with polysemous expressions, in conjunction with copredication, places restrictions on how the referents of these expressions must be individuated. Here, too, we have laid out the evidence in favour of adding structure to semantics in order to resolve this puzzle, specifically, that common nouns carry information relating to the way(s) in which they can be individuated. For both puzzles, we considered alternatives that eschew the adding of structure to semantics and, instead, essentially bleach information out of the semantics and push the complexity into the pragmatics. In either case, however, the conclusion is that one must address structure somewhere (see, e.g., Recanati, 2010). We have provided some reasons for favouring enrichment over impoverishment. Moreover, it does not seem to us that invoking pragmatics as the wastebasket of phenomena that cannot be given an explicit formal account will solve the issues: a properly constrained framework that looks at linguistic phenomena as grounded in cognitive capacities and social practices eliminates the need for a separate pragmatics module or performance mechanisms that somehow override statically encoded meanings.

4 Summary: Adding Structure to Semantics?

Far and away the most widely used semantic theory is based upon a simple type theory (usually the simply-typed λ-calculus), giving rise to the kinds of structures familiar to all those working in the field, namely, sets of possible worlds or situations as the extensions of declarative sentences, functions from worlds to sets of entities or eventualities for common nouns and verbal predicates and so on. There are, however, well-studied alternatives, the underpinnings of which are, non-mutually exclusively, richer type theories on the one hand and frame-based representations on the other. In spite of our individual preferences, we have endeavoured to remain neutral between these two options, and the different ways that each of them has been implemented. With respect to type theory, much work has been based upon (or is in reaction to) Ranta's (1994b) semantics grounded in Martin-Löf's type theory. This in part amounts to the embracing of a different, more fine-grained notion of proposition: one with more structure that is intensional and psychologically realistic. For instance, following the propositions-as-types hypothesis, the interpretations of utterances of declarative sentences (propositions) can be modelled as (arbitrarily) complex types, embedded in the context of the judgements established in a context. Moreover, in these accounts, the link between agents and types (including those that play the role of propositions in the theory) is expressed via the notion of *judgement*, a form of action or inferential move. Regarding frames, the attribute-value structure of a frame allows for a wide array of lexical semantic information and conceptual structure at the sublexical level to be included. For instance, common nouns can be understood to convey not only information regarding their extension but, additionally, at least for count nouns, how the entities they apply to can be individuated. Verb meanings can be broken down into their conceptual constituents, all expressed via a frame structure (or within a richer type theory, or a combination of both).

We have focussed on two topics that cover different facets of developing a semantic theory for realistic language use: the attitudes (propositional contents, the relations between individuals and propositions, mental state attributions), and polysemy and copredication (lexical semantics and interrelated senses of single lexical items). For each, we have reviewed the challenges and problems that arise for simply structured semantic theories and standard views on the division of linguistic subdisciplines.

For the attitudes we discussed theories that model attitude states as structured objects and define the truth of an attitude report in relation to this. The structure enables us to deal with recalcitrant problems with reference in the attitudes, including cases of intentional anaphora where no reference to any actual object is involved. Treating propositions as structured objects such as types enables us to avoid some old problems with the classical view in formal semantics of propositions as sets of possible worlds.

For polysemy and copredication, we laid out the challenges for simply structured semantic accounts posed by the use of polysemous expressions, specifically, accounting for multiple interrelated senses within a single lexical entry, copredication, and the restrictions imposed by combining copredication with quantification (i.e., double-distinctness readings). To our knowledge, there is no proposal that adequately deals with these phenomena without substantially revising the simply-typed underpinnings of semantic theory in the Montagovian tradition. We concluded, in this section, that although a strategy of greatly impoverishing structure in semantics in order to deal with these data cannot be ruled out, there are compelling reasons to allow for a more richly structured semantics at least in terms of types, and, relatedly, also in terms of the amount of information contained in the lexicon, specifically, information regarding individuation criteria.

A topic we have not discussed in depth in this Element is the role of structure in *dialogue* (i.e., distributed and flexible fine-grained structures and mechanisms for capturing the various interrelated factors that explain the efficiency of language underpinning interaction and coordination). Instead, we wish to point readers to an Element devoted to structure in semantics in the light of analysing dialogical phenomena: Gregoromichelaki et al.[39] There, we argue that, for dialogue, a combination of the strategies discussed here for introducing structure needs to be included and extended in that types or frames are required for capturing the intricate interrelations of all domains pertaining to language use beyond the standard distinctions involving lexicon, syntax, semantics, pragmatics, processing and perception/action models. Given that types can be construed as the basis of structuring perception/action for interacting agents and their environment, a realistic conception of types as features of the world–agent relations can be used as the underpinning of a theory of affordances even under a strict Gibsonian direct perception and attunement interpretation. Moreover, if, at the fundamental level, the ontology of the world consists of processes (Bickhard, 2021; Rovelli, 2021), rather than objects/substances, type-theoretic constructs can be seen as the formative underpinning of inferential relations that agents pick up on during language use.

An important feature of the theories we have discussed here is that they introduce structure into the semantics in a general way which then can be applied to the solution of different puzzles. This structure might be provided by a type-theoretic language or the inherent structure of record types or frames. Providing a structured basis for semantic theorising is, in our view, a more principled approach than the introduction of, say, structured meanings to deal specifically

---

[39] Forthcoming (see n. 4 for details).

with the problems of intensionality associated with the attitudes, verbal reports (quotation) or metalinguistic phenomena. Thus, the theories we have presented here provide an overarching theory of structure in semantics which is different from adding certain kinds of structure to solve particular problems. In this way, we feel that these theories provide a potentially general explanatory account of language use and, as such, demonstrate the importance of structure for semantic analysis.

References

Asher, N. (2011). *Lexical Meaning in Context: A Web of Words*. Cambridge University Press. doi.org/10.1017/CBO9780511793936.

Asher, N., & Luo, Z. (2012). Formalisation of coercions in lexical semantics. In E. Chemla, V. Homer & G. Winterstein (Eds.), *Proceedings of Sinn und Bedeutung 17* (pp. 63–80). Retrieved from https://ojs.ub.uni-konstanz.de/sub/index.php/sub/article/view/335 (accessed 2 February 2025).

Asher, N., & Pustejovsky, J. (2006). A type composition logic for generative lexicon. *Journal of Cognitive Science*, 7(1), 1–38. (Reprinted in J. Pustejovsky, P. Bouillon, H. Isahara, K. Kanzaki & C. Lee (Eds.) (2013), *Advances in Generative Lexicon Theory* (pp. 39–66). Springer.)

Babonnaud, W., Kallmeyer, L., & Osswald, R. (2016). Polysemy and coercion: A frame-based approach using LTAG and hybrid logic. In M. Amblard, P. de Groote, S. Pogodalla & C. Retoré (Eds.), *Logical Aspects of Computational Linguistics: Celebrating 20 Years of LACL (1996–2016) – 9th International Conference, LACL 2016*, Lecture Notes in Computer Science LNCS 10054 (pp. 18–33). Springer.

Bach, E. (1986). The algebra of events. *Linguistics and Philosophy*, 9(1), 5–16.

Balogh, K., & Osswald, R. (2021). A frame-based analysis of verbal particles in Hungarian. In S. Löbner, T. Gamerschlag, T. Kalenscher, M. Schrenk & H. Zeevat (Eds.), *Concepts, Frames and Cascades in Semantics, Cognition and Ontology* (pp. 219–237). Springer International. doi.org/10.1007/978-3-030-50200-3_11.

Barner, D., & Snedeker, J. (2005). Quantity judgments and individuation: Evidence that mass nouns count. *Cognition*, 97, 41–66.

Barsalou, L. W. (1992). Frames, concepts, and conceptual fields. In E. Kittay & A. Lehrer (Eds.), *Frames, Fields, and Contrasts: New Essays in Semantic and Lexical Organization* (pp. 21–74). Erlbaum.

Barwise, J., & Cooper, R. (1981). Generalized quantifiers and natural language. *Linguistics and Philosophy*, 4(2), 159–219. doi.org/10.1007/BF00350139.

Bassac, C., Mery, B., & Retoré, C. (2010). Towards a type-theoretical account of lexical semantics. *Journal of Logic, Language and Information*, 19(2), 229–245.

References

Bekki, D. (2018). Introduction to Dependent Type Semantics. In S. Awodey, J. Grudzinska, M. Zawadowski & C. Zwanziger (Eds.), *New Type Theoretic Tools in Natural Language Semantics*. Course, part of North American Summer School Logic, Language, and Information (NASSLLI 2018). Description and slides available at colinzwanziger.com/nasslli-course/ (accessed 1 February 2025).

Bickhard, M. H. (2021). Emergent mental phenomena. In R. W. Clowes, K. Gärtner & I. Hipólito (Eds.), *The Mind-Technology Problem: Investigating Minds, Selves and 21st Century Artefacts* (pp. 49–63). Springer.

Carlson, G. N. (1977). Reference to kinds in English. Unpublished doctoral dissertation, University of Massachusetts at Amherst.

Carnap, R. (1956). *Meaning and Necessity: A Study in Semantics and Modal Logic* (2nd ed.). University of Chicago Press.

Carpenter, B. (1997). *Type-Logical Semantics*. MIT Press.

Champollion, L. (2017). *Parts of a Whole: Distributivity as a Bridge between Aspect and Measurement* (Vol. 66). Oxford University Press.

Champollion, L., & Krifka, M. (2016). Mereology. In M. Aloni (Ed.), *The Cambridge Handbook of Formal Semantics* (pp. 513–541). Cambridge University Press. doi.org/10.1017/cbo9781139236157.014.

Chatzikyriakidis, S., & Luo, Z. (2015a). Individuation criteria, dot-types and copredication: A view from modern type theories. In M. Kuhlmann, M. Kanazawa & G. M. Kobele (Eds.), *Proceedings of the 14th Meeting on the Mathematics of Language (MoL 2015)* (pp. 39–50). Association for Computational Linguistics. doi.org/10.3115/v1/W15-2304.

Chatzikyriakidis, S., & Luo, Z. (2015b). Using signatures in type theory to represent situations. In T. Murata, K. Mineshima & D. Bekki (Eds.), *New Frontiers in Artificial Intelligence: JSAI-isAI 2014 Workshops, LENLS, JURISIN, and GABA, Kanagawa, Japan, October 27–28, 2014, Revised Selected Papers* (Vol. 9067). Springer.

Chatzikyriakidis, S., & Luo, Z. (2018). Identity criteria of common nouns and dot-types for copredication. *Oslo Studies in Language*, *10*(2), 121–141.

Chatzikyriakidis, S., & Luo, Z. (2020). *Formal Semantics in Modern Type Theories*. Wiley.

Chen, L., Kallmeyer, L., & Osswald, R. (2022). A frame-based model of inherent polysemy, copredication and argument coercion. In M. Zock, E. Chersoni, Y.-Y. Hsu & E. Santus (Eds.), *Proceedings of the 7th Workshop on Cognitive Aspects of the Lexicon* (pp. 58–67). Association for Computational Linguistics.

Chierchia, G. (1998). Plurality of mass nouns and the notion of 'semantic parameter'. In S. Rothstein (Ed.), *Events and Grammar. Studies in Linguistics and Philosophy* Vol. 70 (pp. 53–103). Kluwer.

Chierchia, G. (2010). Mass nouns, vagueness and semantic variation. *Synthese, 174*, 99–149.

Chierchia, G. (2015). How universal is the mass/count distinction? Three grammars of counting. In A. Li, A. Simpson & W.- T. D. Tsai (Eds.), *Chinese Syntax: A Cross-Linguistic Perspective* (pp. 147–177). Oxford University Press.

Chierchia, G., & Turner, R. (1988). Semantics and property theory. *Linguistics and Philosophy, 11*, 261–302.

Chomsky, N. (2000). *New Horizons in the Study of Language and Mind*. Cambridge University Press.

Church, A. (1940). A formulation of the simple theory of types. *Journal of Symbolic Logic, 5*(1), 56–68.

Collins, J. (2017). The copredication argument. *Inquiry, 7*, 675–702.

Cooper, R. (2011). Copredication, quantification and frames. In S. Pogodalla & J.- P. Prost (Eds.), *Logical Aspects of Computational Linguistics: 6th International Conference, LACL 2011*, Lecture Notes in Artificial Intelligence LNAI 6736 (pp. 64–79). Springer.

Cooper, R. (2016). Frames as records. In A. Foret, G. Morrill, R. Muskens, R. Osswald & S. Pogodalla (Eds.), *Formal Grammar: 20th and 21st International Conferences FG 2015, Barcelona, Spain, August 2015, Revised Selected Papers FG 2016, Bozen, Italy, August 2016, Proceedings* (pp. 3–18). Springer.

Cooper, R. (2023). *From Perception to Communication: A Theory of Types for Action and Meaning*. Oxford University Press.

Cresswell, M. J. (1985). *Structured Meanings: The Semantics of Propositional Attitudes*. MIT Press.

Davidson, D. (1969/1980). The individuation of events. In N. Rescher (Ed.), *Essays in Honor of Carl G. Hempel* (pp. 216–234). Springer.

De Jaegher, H., & Di Paolo, E. (2007). Participatory sense-making: An enactive approach to social cognition. *Phenomenology and the Cognitive Sciences, 6*(4), 485–507. doi.org/10.1007/s11097-007-9076-9.

Dowty, D. (1991). Thematic proto-roles and argument selection. *Language, 67*(3), 547–619.

Filip, H. (1993/1999). Aspect, situation types and noun phrase semantics. PhD thesis, University of California at Berkeley, 1993. Published in 1999 as *Aspect, Eventuality Types and Noun Phrase Semantics*. Garland.

Fillmore, C. J. (1976). Frame semantics and the nature of language. *Annals of the New York Academy of Sciences, 280*(1), 20–32.

Fillmore, C. J. (1977). Topics in lexical semantics. In R. Cole (Ed.), *Current Issues in Linguistic Theory* (pp. 76–138). Indiana University Press.

Fillmore, C. J. (1982). Frame semantics. In the Linguistic Society of Korea (Ed.), *Linguistics in the Morning Calm: Selected papers from SICOL 1981*. Hanshin.

Francez, N., & Dyckhoff, R. (2010). Proof-theoretic semantics for a natural language fragment. *Linguistics and Philosophy, 33*, 447–477.

Gallin, D. (1975). *Intensional and Higher-Order Modal Logic*. North-Holland.

Geach, P. T. (1967). Intentional identity. *Journal of Philosophy, 64*(20), 627–632.

Ginzburg, J. (2012). *The Interactive Stance: Meaning for Conversation*. Oxford University Press.

Ginzburg, J., & Cooper, R. (2004). Clarification, ellipsis, and the nature of contextual updates in dialogue. *Linguistics and Philosophy, 27*(3), 297–365.

Gotham, M. (2014). Copredication, quantification and individuation. Unpublished doctoral dissertation, University College London.

Gotham, M. (2017). Composing criteria of individuation in copredication. *Journal of Semantics, 34*(2), 333–371. doi.org/10.1093/jos/ffw008.

Gotham, M. (2021). Property inheritance, deferred reference and copredication. *Journal of Semantics, 39*(1), 87–116. doi.org/10.1093/jos/ffab020.

Gregoromichelaki, E., Chatzikyriakidis, S., Eshghi, A., Hough, J., Howes, C., Kempson, R., Kiaer, J., Purver, M., Sadrzadeh, M., & White, G. (2020). Affordance competition in dialogue: The case of syntactic universals. In *Proceedings of the 24th Workshop on the Semantics and Pragmatics of Dialogue – Full Papers*. SEMDIAL. Retrieved from http://semdial.org/anthology/Z20-Gregoromichelaki_semdial_0022.pdf (accessed 1 February 2025).

Gregoromichelaki, E., Kempson, R., Purver, M., Mills, G., Cann, R., Meyer-Viol, W., & Healey, P. (2011). Incrementality and intention-recognition in utterance processing. *Dialogue and Discourse: Special Issue on Incremental Processing in Dialogue, 2*(1), 199–233.

Groenendijk, J., & Stokhof, M. (1990). Dynamic Montague Grammar. In L. Kalman & L. Polos (Eds.), *Proceedings of the 2nd Symposium on Logic and Language* (pp. 3–48). Budapest.

Harper, R., Honsell, F., & Plotkin, G. (1993). A framework for defining logics. *Journal of the Association for Computing Machinery, 40*(1), 143–184.

Hintikka, J. (1962). *Knowledge and Belief: An Introduction to the Logic of Two Notions*. Cornell University Press.

Jakubíček, M., Kilgarriff, A., Kovář, V., Rychlý, P., & Suchomel, V. (2013). The TenTen corpus family. In A. Hardie & R. Love (Eds.), *Corpus Linguistics 2013: Abstract Book*, papers from the 7th international Corpus Linguistics conference (CL2013) at Lancaster University (pp. 125–127). UCREL. https://ucrel.lancs.ac.uk/cl2013/doc/CL2013-ABSTRACT-BOOK.pdf (accessed 2 February 2025).

Kallmeyer, L., Lichte, T., Osswald, R., Pogodalla, S., & Wurm, C. (2015). Quantification in frame semantics with hybrid logic. In R. Cooper & C. Retoré (Eds.), *TYTLES: TYpe Theory and LExical Semantics*, papers from the European Summer School in Logic, Language and Information (ESSLLI 2015) in Barcelona. www.lirmm.fr/tytles/Articles/Kallmeyer.pdf (accessed 2 February 2025).

Kallmeyer, L., & Osswald, R. (2017). Modeling quantification with polysemous nouns. In C. Gardent & C. Retoré (Eds.), *Proceedings of the 12th International Conference on Computational Semantics (IWCS 2017) – Short Papers*. https://aclanthology.org/W17-6914.pdf (accessed 2 February 2025).

Kamp, H. (1990). Prolegomena to a structural theory of belief and other attitudes. In C. A. Anderson & J. Owens (Eds.), *Propositional Attitudes: The Role of Content in Logic, Language and Mind*. CSLI Publications.

Kamp, H. (2022). Referential and attributive descriptions. In D. Altshuler (Ed.), *Linguistics Meets Philosophy* (pp. 77–108). Cambridge University Press. doi.org/10.1017/9781108766401.006.

Kamp, H., & Reyle, U. (1993). *From Discourse to Logic*. Kluwer.

Kamp, H., van Genabith, J., & Reyle, U. (2011). Discourse representation theory. In D. Gabbay & F. Guenthner (Eds.), *Handbook of Philosophical Logic* (Vol. 15). Springer Science+Business Media. doi.org/10.1007/978-94-007-0485-5_3.

Kilgarriff, A., Rychlý, P., Smrz, P., & Tugwell, D. (2004). The sketch engine. In G. Williams & S. Vessier (Eds.), *11th EURALEX International Congress* (pp. 105–115). Université de Bretagne-Sud, Faculté des lettres et des sciences humaines.

Kohlhase, M. (1992). Unification in order-sorted type theory. In A. Voronkov (Ed.), *Proceedings of the International Conference on Logic Programming and Automated Reasoning LPAR'92 (LNAI 624)* (pp. 421–432). Springer.

Kohlhase, M. (1994). A mechanization of sorted higher-order logic based on the resolution principle. Unpublished doctoral dissertation, Universität des Saarlandes, Germany.

Kratzer, A. (2022). Attitude ascriptions and speech reports. In D. Altshuler (Ed.), *Linguistics Meets Philosophy* (pp. 17–50). Cambridge University Press. doi.org/10.1017/9781108766401.

Krifka, M. (1986). Nominalreferenz und Zeitkonstitution: Zur Semantik von Massentermen, Pluraltermen und Aspektklassen, Unpublished doctoral dissertation, Universität München.

Krifka, M. (1989). Nominal reference, temporal constitution and quantification in event semantics. In R. Bartsch, J. F. A. K. v. Benthem, & P. v. E. Boas (Eds.), *Semantics and Contextual Expression* (pp. 75–115). Foris.

Kripke, S. (1977). Speaker's reference and semantic reference. *Midwest Studies in Philosophy*, 255–276.

Landman, F. (1991). *Structures for Semantics*. Studies in Linguistics and Philosophy, Vol. 45. Kluwer.

Landman, F. (2011). Count nouns – mass nouns – neat nouns – mess nouns. *Baltic International Yearbook of Cognition*, *6*, 1–67.

Landman, F. (2016). Iceberg semantics for count nouns and mass nouns: Classifiers, measures and portions. *Baltic International Yearbook of Cognition*, *11*, 1–48.

Lecomte, A., & Retoré, C. (1998). Words as modules: A lexicalised grammar in the framework of linear logic proof nets. In C. Martín-Vide (Ed.), *Mathematical and Computational Analysis of Natural Language: Selected Papers from the 2nd International Conference on Mathematical Linguistics (ICML '96), Tarragona, 1996* (pp. doi.org/10.1075/sfsl.45, 129–144). John Benjamins.

Lewis, D. (1970). General semantics. *Synthese*, *22*(1–2), 18–67. doi.org/10.1007/ BF00413598.

Lewis, D. (1979). Attitudes de dicto and de se. *Philosophical Review*, *88*, 513–543. (Reprinted in Lewis, 1983.)

Lewis, D. (1983). *Philosophical Papers, Volume 1*. Oxford University Press

Lewis, D. (1991). *Parts of Classes*. Blackwell.

Liebesman, D., & Magidor, O. (2017). Copredication and property inheritance. *Philosophical Issues*, *27*, 131–166.

Liebesman, D., & Magidor, O. (2019). Copredication, counting, and criteria of individuation: A response to Gotham. *Journal of Semantics*, *36*, 549–561.

Liefke, K. (2014). A single-type semantics for natural language. Unpublished doctoral dissertation, Tilburg University, Center for Logic and Philosophy of Science.

Liefke, K. (2024). *Natural Language Ontology and Semantic Theory*. Cambridge University Press.

Liefke, K., & Werning, M. (2018). Evidence for single-type semantics: An alternative to *e*/*t*-based dual-type semantics. *Journal of Semantics*, *35*(4), 639–685. doi.org/10.1093/jos/ffy009.

Link, G. (1983). The logical analysis of plurals and mass terms: A lattice-theoretic approach. In R. Bäuerle, C. Schwarze & A. von Stechow (Eds.), *Meaning, Use and the Interpretation of Language* (pp. 303–323). Walter de Gruyter. (Reprinted in P. Portner & B. H. Partee (Eds.) (2002), *Formal Semantics: The Essential Readings* (pp. 127–146). Blackwell.)

Löbner, S. (2014). Evidence for frames from human language. In T. Gamerschlag, D. Gerland, R. Osswald & W. Petersen (Eds.), *Frames and Concept Types: Applications in Language and Philosophy* (pp. 23–67). Springer.

Löbner, S. (2015). Functional concepts and frames. In T. Gamerschlag, D. Gerland, R. Osswald & W. Petersen (Eds.), *Meaning, Frames, and Conceptual Representation* (pp. 15–42). Düsseldorf University Press.

Luo, Z. (1999). Coercive subtyping. *Journal of Logic and Computation*, *9*(1), 105–130.

Luo, Z. (2010). Type-theoretical semantics with coercive subtyping. In N. Li & D. Lutz (Eds.), *Proceedings of Semantics and Linguistic Theory (SALT) 20* (pp. 38–56). CLC Publications at Cornell University. https://journals.linguisticsociety.org/proceedings/index.php/SALT/article/view/2580/2328 (accessed 2 February 2025).

Luo, Z. (2011). Contextual analysis of word meanings in type-theoretical semantics. In S. Pogodalla & J.-P. Prost (Eds.), *Logical Aspects of Computational Linguistics: 6th International Conference, LACL 2011*, Lecture Notes in Artificial Intelligence LNAI 6736 (pp. 159–174). Springer.

Luo, Z. (2014). Formal semantics in modern type theories: Is it model-theoretic, proof-theoretic, or both? In N. Asher & S. Soloviev (Eds.), *Logical Aspects of Computational Linguistics: 8th International Conference, LACL 2014*, Lecture Notes in Computer Science LNCS 8535 (pp. 177–188). Springer.

Maier, E. (2017). Referential dependencies between conflicting attitudes. *Journal of Philosophical Logic*, *46*(2), 141–167. doi.org/10.1007/s10992-016-9397-7.

Martin-Löf, P. (1982). Constructive mathematics and computer programming. In L. J. Cohen, J. Łoś, H. Pfeiffer & K.- P. Podewski (Eds.), *Logic, Methodology and Philosophy of Science VI: Proceedings of the Sixth International Congress of Logic, Methodology and Philosophy of Science, Hannover, 1979*. Studies in Logic and the Foundations of Mathematics, Vol. 104 (pp. 153–175). North-Holland. doi.org/10.1016/S0049-237X(09)70189-2.

Martin-Löf, P. (1984). *Intuitionistic Type Theory*. Bibliopolis.

Martin-Löf, P. (1996). On the meanings of the logical constants and the justifications of the logical laws. *Nordic Journal of Philosophical Logic*, 1(1), 11–60.

Montague, R. (1970). Universal grammar. *Theoria*, 36, 373–398.

Montague, R. (1973). The proper treatment of quantification in ordinary English. In J. Hintikka, J. Moravcsik & P. Suppes (Eds.), *Approaches to Natural Language: Proceedings of the 1970 Stanford Workshop on Grammar and Semantics* (pp. 247–270). D. Reidel.

Montague, R. (1974). *Formal Philosophy: Selected Papers of Richard Montague*. Yale University Press. (Edited and with an introduction by Richmond H. Thomason.)

Muskens, R. (1996). Combining Montague semantics and discourse representation. *Linguistics and Philosophy*, 19(2), 143–186.

Nordström, B., Petersson, K., & Smith, J. M. (1990). *Programming in Martin-Löf's Type Theory* (Vol. 7). Clarendon Press.

Nunberg, G. (1979). The non-uniqueness of semantic solutions: Polysemy. *Linguistics and Philosophy*, 3(2), 143–184.

Ortega-Andrés, M., & Vicente, A. (2019). Polysemy and co-predication. *Glossa*, 4(1), article 1, 1–23. doi.org/10.5334/gjgl.564.

Osswald, R., & Van Valin, R. D. (2014). FrameNet, frame structure, and the syntax-semantics interface. In T. Gamerschlag, D. Gerland, R. Osswald & W. Petersen (Eds.), *Frames and Concept Types: Applications in Language and Philosophy* (pp. 125–156). Springer. doi.org/10.1007/978-3-319-01541-5_6.

Parsons, T. (1990). *Events in the Semantics of English*. MIT Press.

Partee, B. (2007). *Type theory and natural language: Do we need two basic types?* Retrieved from http://people.umass.edu/partee/docs/TwoTypesHOMarch07.pdf (accessed 2 February 2025). (100th Meeting of the Seminar: Mathematical Methods Applied to Linguistics, Moscow State University.)

Petersen, W. (2015). Representation of concepts as frames. In T. Gamerschlag, D. Gerland, R. Osswald & W. Petersen (Eds.), *Meaning, Frames, and Conceptual Representation* (pp. 43–67). Düsseldorf University Press.

(Commented reprint of Petersen, W. (2007). Representation of concepts as frames. In J. Skilters, F. Toccafondi & G. Stemberger (Eds.), *Complex Cognition and Qualitative Science*. Volume 2 of the *Baltic International Yearbook of Cognition, Logic and Communication*, pp. 151–170. University of Latvia.)

Petersen, W., & Werning, M. (2007). Conceptual fingerprints: Lexical decomposition by means of frames – a neuro-cognitive model. In U. Priss, S. Polovina & R. Hill (Eds.), *Conceptual Structures: Knowledge Architectures for Smart Applications* (pp. 415–428). Springer. doi.org/10.1007/978-3-540-73681-3_31.

Pietroski, P. (2003). The character of natural language semantics. In A. Barber (Ed.), *Epistemology of Language* (pp. 217–256). Oxford University Press.

Pross, T. (2014). *Fodor's puzzle and the semantics of attitude reports*. Retrieved from www.ims.uni-stuttgart.de/documents/team/prosstn/files/pross-attitudes.pdf (accessed 2 February 2025).

Pustejovsky, J. (1995). *The Generative Lexicon*. MIT Press.

Pustejovsky, J. (2008). From concepts to meaning: The role of lexical knowledge. In P. van Sterkenburg (Ed.), *Unity and Diversity of Languages* (pp. 73–84). John Benjamins. doi.org/10.1075/z.141.08pus.

Pustejovsky, J. (2011). Coercion in a general theory of argument selection. *Linguistics*, *49*(6), 1401–1431.

Quine, W. (1960). *Word and Object: An Inquiry into the Linguistic Mechanisms of Objective Reference*. John Wiley.

Ranta, A. (1988). Propositions as games as types. *Synthese*, *76*(3), 377–395.

Ranta, A. (1991). Intuitionistic categorial grammar. *Linguistics and Philosophy*, *14*(2), 203–239.

Ranta, A. (1994a). Syntactic categories in the language of mathematics. In P. Dybjer, B. Nordström & J. Smith (Eds.), *Types for Proofs and Programs: International Workshop TYPES '94*. Lecture Notes in Computer Science LNCS 996 (pp. 162–182). Springer.

Ranta, A. (1994b). *Type-Theoretical Grammar*. Clarendon Press.

Ranta, A. (1994c). Type theory and the informal language of mathematics. In P. Dybjer, B. Nordström & J. Smith (Eds.), *Types for Proofs and Programs: International Workshop TYPES '94*. Lecture Notes in Computer Science LNCS 996 (pp. 352–365). Springer.

Recanati, F. (2010). *Truth-Conditional Pragmatics*. Oxford University Press. doi.org/10.1093/acprof:oso/9780199226993.001.0001.

Retoré, C. (2014). The Montagovian generative lexicon ΛTy_n: A type theoretical framework for natural language semantics. In R. Matthes & A. Schubert (Eds.), *Types for Proofs and Programs: LIPIcs Proceedings*

19th International Conference TYPES 2013, April 22–26, 2013, Toulouse, France. Books on Demand. Retrieved from https://books.google.se/books?id=ohEtBAAAQBAJ (accessed 2 February 2025).

Rett, J. (2022). A typology of semantic entities. In D. Altshuler (Ed.), *Linguistics Meets Philosophy* (pp. 277–301). Cambridge University Press. doi.org/10.1017/9781108766401.

Rothstein, S. (2010). Counting and the mass/count distinction. *Journal of Semantics*, 27(3), 343–397.

Rovelli, C. (2021). *Helgoland: The Strange and Beautiful Story of Quantum Physics*. Penguin Books.

Russell, B. (1903). *Principles of Mathematics*. Norton.

Searle, J. (1980). The background of meaning. In J. R. Searle, F. Kiefer, and M. Bierwisch (Eds.), *Speech Act Theory and Pragmatics* (pp. 221–232). Springer.

Soames, S. (1987). Direct reference, propositional attitudes, and semantic content. *Philosophical Topics*, 15(1), 47–87. doi.org/10.5840/philtopics198715112.

Sundholm, G. (1986). Proof theory and meaning. In D. Gabbay & F. Guenthner (Eds.), *Handbook of Philosophical Logic, Vol. III*. Reidel.

Sundholm, G. (1989). Constructive generalized quantifiers. *Synthese*, 79, 1–12.

Sutton, P. R. (2022). Restrictions on copredication: A situation theoretic approach. *Semantics and Linguistic Theory (SALT)*, 32, 335–355.

Sutton, P. R. (2024). Individuation criteria and copredication: Modification in context. In G. Baumann, D. Gutzmann, J. Koopman, K. Liefke, A. Renans & T. Scheffler (Eds.), *Proceedings of Sinn und Bedeutung. 28* (pp. 876–894). doi.org/10.18148/sub/2024.v28.1167.

Sutton, P. R., & Filip, H. (2016). Vagueness, overlap, and countability. In N. Bade, P. Berezovskaya & A. Schöller (Eds.), *Proceedings of Sinn und Bedeutung 20* (pp. 730–747). Retrieved from https://ojs.ub.uni-konstanz.de/sub/index.php/sub/article/view/292/226 (accessed 2 February 2025).

Sutton, P. R., & Filip, H. (2017). Individuation, reliability, and the mass/count distinction. *Journal of Language Modelling*, 5(2), 303–356.

Sutton, P. R., & Filip, H. (2020). Informational object nouns and the mass/count distinction. In M. Franke, N. Kompa, M. Liu, J. L. Mueller & J. Schwab (Eds.), *Proceedings of Sinn und Bedeutung 24*, 2, 319–335. doi.org/10.18148/sub/2020.v24i2.900.

Sutton, P. R., & Filip, H. (2021). Container, portion, and measure interpretations of pseudo-partitive constructions. In T. Kiss, F. J. Pelletier & H. Husić (Eds.), *Things and Stuff: The Semantics of the Count-Mass Distinction* (pp. 279–304). Cambridge University Press.

van Benthem, J. (1990). Categorial grammar and type theory. *Journal of Philosophical Logic*, *19*(2), 115–168.

Weinreich, U. (1964). On the semantic structure of language. In J. H. Greenberg (Ed.), *Universals of Language.* MIT Press.

Xue, T., & Luo, Z. (2012). Dot-types and their implementation. In D. Béchet and A. Dikovsky (Eds.), *International Conference on Logical Aspects of Computational Linguistics* (pp. 234–249). Springer.

Acknowledgements

Stergios Chatzikyriakidis' research was supported by the grant LaM (Language and Meaning: A Natural Language Understanding Platform for Greek), funded by the Special Account for Research Grants (SARG) at the University of Crete and from the European Union under Horizon Europe (TALOS-AI4SSH 101087269).

Robin Cooper's research was supported by Vetenskapsrådet project 2014-39 for the establishment of the Centre for Linguistic Theory and Studies in Probability (CLASP) at the University of Gothenburg.

Peter Sutton's research was supported by the Beatriu de Pinós postdoctoral fellowships programme, funded by the Secretary of Universities and Research (Government of Catalonia) and from the Horizon 2020 programme of research and innovation of the European Union under the Marie Skłodowska-Curie grant agreement no. 801370.

Funding for the open access publication of this Element was provided by the Centre for Linguistic Theory and Studies in Probability (CLASP) and the Section for Linguistics both at the Department of Philosophy, Linguistics and Theory of Science, University of Gothenburg.

Contributors

All four authors were involved in the writing of all sections. However, the main author responsible for Section 2 was Cooper, and for Section 3, Chatzikyriakidis and Sutton.

Semantics

Jonathan Ginzburg
Université Paris-Cité

Jonathan Ginzburg is Professor of Linguistics at Université Paris-Cité (formerly Paris 7). He has held appointments at the Hebrew University of Jerusalem and King's College, London. He is one of the founders and currently associate editor of the journal *Dialogue and Discourse*. His research interests include semantics, dialogue, and language acquisition. He is the author of *Interrogative Investigations* (CSLI Publications, 2001, with Ivan A. Sag) and *The Interactive Stance: Meaning for Conversation* (Oxford University Press, 2012).

Daniel Lassiter
University of Edinburgh

Daniel Lassiter is Senior Lecturer in Semantics in Linguistics & English Language at the University of Edinburgh. He works on topics at the intersection of formal semantics/pragmatics, cognitive psychology, and philosophy of language, including modality, conditionals, vagueness, scalar semantics, and Bayesian pragmatics. He is the author of *Graded Modality* (Oxford University Press, 2017) and numerous journal articles.

About the Series

Elements in Semantics emphasizes the field's recent flourishing of interdisciplinary work, connecting linguistics and philosophy with cognitive science, computer science, neuroscience, law, anthropology, sociology, economics, and beyond. The series should be of interest to a broad community of researchers interested in the study of meaning from diverse perspectives.

Cambridge Elements

Semantics

Elements in the Series

Natural Language Ontology and Semantic Theory
Kristina Liefke

Reduction and Unification in Natural Language Ontology
Kristina Liefke

Semantics and Deep Learning
Lasha Abzianidze, Lisa Bylinina, and Denis Paperno

Types and the Structure of Meaning: Issues in Compositional and Lexical Semantics
Stergios Chatzikyriakidis, Robin Cooper, Eleni Gregoromichelaki and Peter R. Sutton

A full series listing is available at: www.cambridge.org/ESEM

For EU product safety concerns, contact us at Calle de José Abascal, 56–1°,
28003 Madrid, Spain or eugpsr@cambridge.org.

www.ingramcontent.com/pod-product-compliance
Ingram Content Group UK Ltd.
Pitfield, Milton Keynes, MK11 3LW, UK
UKHW022244220326
469255UK00019B/355